Home Improvement

How to Improve and Maintain Every Area of Your Home

(Everything You Need to Know About Construction Contracts Estimating Planning and Scheduling)

Brian Skinner

Published By **Bengion Cosalas**

Brian Skinner

All Rights Reserved

Home Improvement: How to Improve and Maintain Every Area of Your Home (Everything You Need to Know About Construction Contracts Estimating Planning and Scheduling)

ISBN 978-1-7780652-2-4

No part of this guidebook shall be reproduced in any form without permission in writing from the publisher except in the case of brief quotations embodied in critical articles or reviews.

Legal & Disclaimer

The information contained in this book is not designed to replace or take the place of any form of medicine or professional medical advice. The information in this book has been provided for educational & entertainment purposes only.

The information contained in this book has been compiled from sources deemed reliable, and it is accurate to the best of the Author's knowledge; however, the Author cannot guarantee its accuracy and validity and cannot be held liable for any errors or omissions. Changes are periodically made to this book. You must consult your doctor or get professional medical advice before using any of the suggested remedies, techniques, or information in this book.

Upon using the information contained in this book, you agree to hold harmless the Author from and against any damages, costs, and expenses, including any legal fees potentially resulting from the application of any of the information provided by this guide. This disclaimer applies to any damages or injury caused by the use and application, whether directly or indirectly, of any advice or information presented, whether for breach of contract, tort, negligence, personal injury, criminal intent, or under any other cause of action.

You agree to accept all risks of using the information presented inside this book. You need to consult a professional medical practitioner in order to ensure you are both able and healthy enough to participate in this program.

Table Of Contents

Chapter 1: The Initial Costs 1

Chapter 2: Return on Investment (ROI) 9

Chapter 3: Environmental Impact 17

Chapter 4: Property Tax Liability 22

Chapter 5: The Benefits of an Addition or Remodel 28

Chapter 6: The Benefits of Tearing Down and Building New 35

Chapter 7: How to Patch a Hole in Your Wall 40

Chapter 8: How to Replace an Outlet or Switch 68

Chapter 9: How to Paint Your Interior 99

Chapter 10: How to Paint Your Exterior 132

Chapter 11: How to Fix or Replace a Leaky Faucet 167

Chapter 1: The Initial Costs

When considering whether or not to tear down and construct a brand new home, or to modify your cutting-edge residence with an addition or redecorate, the primary issue that you'll be wanting to take into account is that of fee. Of course there is more to charge than genuinely the amount of cash you pay for substances and difficult artwork, and therefore you may want to sit down down down along side your architect or contractor to make certain your charge range is entire earlier than jumping to a quick end.

For instance, normally materials and hard art work are considered "tough fees," and yet a fantastic percentage of various prices called "mild prices" need to be factored in as well. Soft charges embody such things as architectural and engineering prices, felony costs, and financing. Not to say, there's the Contractor's "modern day situations" (water, transient power, jobsite workplaces, storage, supervision, and verbal exchange); and of route your private relocation expenses assuming you may be no longer able to stay in your house for the duration of introduction. General Conditions and relocation fees usually relate to the undertaking schedule, due to the truth, for instance, the longer the task takes, the more time the Contractor will need a short relaxation room on net web page (simply an example), and the longer you will be staying inside the Holiday Inn.

According to research, and understandably so, beginning from scratch and constructing a ultra-modern house is normally less expensive in case you study it at the idea of dollar constant with square foot, in desire to a redecorate or addition undertaking. This is because of the truth even as one is building a residence from scratch, the whole lot is completed in a coordinated way to permit for maximum overall performance. Not to say the financial device of scale. From the inspiration to the wall finishes, electric powered wiring to the quilt plates, the whole lot can be sequenced meticulously therefore enhancing average performance every step of the way. On the opportunity, adding directly to or reworking your present day residence constrains you to an present framework and often instances the sequencing may additionally therefore be dictated by using the usage of an present day state of affairs.

While reworking and including directly to an existing house can also seem like a small task ("seem" is the key word right here), the reality of the problem is that it is generally suddenly an prolonged task, and further high-priced at the surrender of the day. Dealing with a cramped web web page and unanticipated defects present in the gift structure with the goal of with the resource of some way developing a big transformation is rarely smooth or less expensive. Also, Contractors normally charge extra to feature at once to and redesign gift homes thinking about the reality that they want to take care of a number of limitations and surprising conditions that they understand they received't be capable of anticipate from the begin, which might be absolutely now not present while building a new home from scratch. Furthermore, in case you are making plans to collect an addition upwards (ie, via manner of such as a 2nd tale as an instance), this can pose a structural challenge while you bear in mind that the unique basis and gravity load assisting structural contributors were in the beginning designed and constructed handiest to help a single story and roof load, and no longer presupposed to guide a 2d tale.

The Size Factor

Although we've already stated that which consist of without delay to or remodeling your contemporary residence may be more costly than constructing a modern day one, there may be a few different aspect of the coin to maintain in thoughts. The significance of your venture must help you make a decision your alternatives in moderate of price to help you make a choice. For instance, if all you want is to honestly demolish one outdoors wall of one room to boom in a single direction, then my fine bet is that it's going to be less difficult and less expensive to do this in place of flattening the entire home and constructing a present day one. Of course that is an apparent example with an clean selection; and most probably you're reading this e book because of the reality your private state of affairs isn't so easy.

Here's every other situation: Let's say you've recently offered an older home that doesn't have a number one bed room or draw near toilet, and you're consequently presently napping in a smaller bedroom and are sharing a hallway toilet together together together with your youngsters who're unhappily sharing a mattress room. You're now searching for to transform the house to make it greater spacious, to create the master suite, and to cut up the youngsters's snoozing areas into two bedrooms. If you have got got sufficient outdoor location (which you don't mind dropping), and the ground plan is arranged such that you can fairly without trouble enlarge with a single story addition in a single course into that outside place, then it's probable that it would be economically prudent to preserve with the addition. However, in case you are hoping to set up the entire floor ground, and pass the kitchen to the other side of the house, combine the smaller bedrooms at the floor ground into a prime bedroom, after which create a current 2nd tale for the kids's bedrooms upstairs – nicely then you've nearly changed the entire house as we're aware of it, and most in all likelihood it's far going to be less complicated, quicker, and lots lots less expensive certainly to begin from scratch.

So, even though it is tough to generalize in text with out the benefit of having a complete expertise of your mission specifics, proper right here's a rule of thumb: If you're looking at a situation in which you need to touch or through some manner alter extra than 60% of the prevailing home, the most prudent factor to do is probable to tear down and construct a cutting-edge residence except there can be some treasured detail of the existing domestic's individual or shape that makes it unique and unique.

The truth of the trouble is that each options (tearing down and building a brand new domestic and adding at once to or remodeling the winning domestic) have blessings and drawbacks. So permit's hold taking area the manner to bear in mind some different factors past the preliminary fees.

Chapter 2: Return on Investment (ROI)

Whether you are undertaking this mission with the save you-recreation objective of promoting your property in the future or now not, it's clever to don't forget the potential go back on investment. When figuring out what to do as you improve your private home, it's important which you ask yourself whether or not or no longer or no longer what you're making plans will growth the charge of your private home, and by the use of how lots. This requires deeper attention and calculations to appearance whether or no longer the stepped forward fee may be sizeable or surely minimum and therefore now not well well worth task. And of path it's satisfactory to try and keep away from spending coins on improvements that would definitely make your property less appealing to capability clients. For instance, maybe you like the shade gold, and want to change all of the chrome steel plumbing furnishings to gold, and paint every room in gold leaf paint, and draw close gold and diamond chandeliers from the ceiling in every room. You may spend a fortune, and probably not get again a penny. That's clearly horrible ROI, and consequently awful preference-making.

It's satisfactory to bear in mind ROI with every agenda and ability financial conditions in mind. In maximum cases, remodeling and along with at once to the winning domestic need to help rework the antique shape into a more valuable investment, specifically if the work is designed with the aid of the use of manner of a professional Architect and constructed with the aid of a certified Contractor with the perfect know-how and experience to adopt the type of assignment. If you're planning to resell your own home after modifying it, you can need to do not forget whether or not the money you make investments into the venture can be recovered after the sale and whether or not or now not it's going to assist you're making a bigger income out of the sale. In many instances, this will be decided through factors together with the location and triumphing market situations, and the price in line with square foot of surrounding "comps" (comparables). It is right to take a seat down down together with your actual belongings agent, or an appraiser, to speak approximately each and each issue concerned as a protracted way as valuation is worried.

If you are dealing with an older house, the wonderful alternative can be to don't forget every desire in light of the destiny, looking at it with more than the subsequent 15 years in thoughts. A unique instance is to maintain in thoughts whether or no longer within the future you (or the following Owner) may additionally additionally need to make in addition changes to the identical residence to decorate its fantastic or to function vicinity. If, as an instance, you desire to transform the indoors finishes of your very vintage house, but the surrounding community homes are 3 times the size and lots extra current, then possibilities are that many ability clients may want to have their eye on your house with the concept of in the long run tearing it down and rebuilding, or increasing onto it substantially. Therefore, putting masses of cash proper proper into a redecorate isn't exactly prudent, and you might be higher off honestly not spending that money because of the fact you'll never see a super return on your investment (ROI).

You will want to do not forget the entirety, which include the situation of the form (you can continually are seeking recommendation from a Structural Engineer if uncertain), the interior wall finishes, the current-day state of the prevailing electric powered powered device, plumbing gadget, and mechanical HVAC device, and another unique competencies there may be to look how they'll be tormented by the remodeling mission, and what a capability client might also reflect onconsideration on their us of a or adjustments they'd need to make. If the probably opinion can be that any maximum important system would want to be gutted and rebuilt, then it may be less complicated to take the route of building a current residence as much as the modern code and building industry requirements in place of transforming. Additionally, if your own home has giant issues, it'll probable be easier to head the tear-down route and then assemble a modern one. This manner you received't be left having to cope with every and each little problem, that can display time-consuming and high-priced. Practical times have demonstrated that no matter the fact that the actual financial fees of tearing down and rebuilding is probably slightly greater expensive as opposed to a redecorate assignment, the elevated appraised value of the house permits the Owner to promote it for notably greater, with a better ROI

I'm guessing you surely understand the idea of ROI by way of manner of manner of now, but honestly to offer you some actual numerical examples, proper right here's a very made-up example scenario: Let's say you simply offered an older house for $two hundred,000, but it's no longer quite massive sufficient to your developing family, and therefore you want to function place.

Option 1: You can assemble an addition into the rear outdoor, a remarkable manner to rate $one hundred,000. At that point, your realtor advises that you can in all likelihood sell the residence (with the extra square pictures) for $350,000 inside the modern-day market. For the sake of simplicity, permit's definitely forget approximately approximately all the promoting expenses, which encompass realtor's fees. In the most effective form of the mathematics, you're looking at a $50,000 pass decrease returned on a $a hundred,000 investment. This is a 50% ROI. Pretty applicable!

Option 2: You can knock down the house, and assemble a today's one – precisely the dimensions you need. This may additionally need to charge $250,000 no matter the fact that, your Architect and Contractor advocate. So you skip talk in your realtor, and he/she tells you that a new house on this network of that period may sell for a lot greater, because of the fact new homes there are in name for and hard to head again via. He/she thinks you can get at the least $500,000 for a new residence as described. Again, ignoring financing expenses and realtor's prices, and masses of others., you're searching at an ROI of $50,000 once more, but this time on a $250,000 investment. Therefore, that is a 20% ROI.

So in each case, you at the least have a powerful ROI, which is right because it technique you're no longer going to lose any cash. But truely, a 50% ROI is better than a 20% ROI, proper? So in this case, an addition is the way to move, regardless of the fact that your house may be properly nicely worth only $350,000 as opposed to $500,000 on the same time as you're finished. Furthermore, you'll quality must give you $a hundred,000 to execute the project, in choice to a whopping $250,000. A bonus!

Chapter 3: Environmental Impact

Another attention that I recommend factoring into your decision making method is that of the effect your task could have on the environment. It is unlucky that many people do now not assume past their private pockets or pocketbook, due to the fact we all have a sure duty to limit bad implications at the environment for the gain of future generations to go back. The accountable and first rate issue to do is to at the least try to find a answer with a purpose to no longer high-quality suit your monetary constraints, but on the identical time restriction environmental results wherein viable. Without harping on why it's crucial to protect the environment, I'll just ask you to preserve in thoughts considering it the identical way you remember balloting in the route of an election. The effect you have got is truly one unmarried vote, which seems minimal, high-quality. But together, each and anybody vote gives as a outstanding deal as make a difference inside the grander scheme. The equal idea applies with environmental obligation. Okay, off my soap-discipline now and shifting without delay to the selection to be had.

It is obvious that the method of constructing a today's home allows you the opportunity of utilizing current day inexperienced constructing structures and technology in place of that of remodeling an present home. In fact, the present day building code will generally require at the least a minimal popular of insulation, green gadget, and twin-pane glazing with awesome solar warm temperature gain ordinary overall performance standards, and lots of others. But alternatively, demolishing an gift residence excellent does create pretty a few useless waste disposal, and also you don't get the advantage of "reusing" materials.

Serious idea must take delivery of to the 2 production alternatives to appearance which one weighs extra on the environment than the opportunity. First, it is crucial to be aware that constructing a new house from scratch is less complex, and can in all likelihood preserve energy in the future. But but, reusing and reworking your vintage residence can be a greener choice relying on what form of splendid sustainable changes you may be able to make to it finally of the reworking method.

All the elements that can be involved are widespread, however variety from venture to project, so all that can be said right here in this e-book is which you want to weigh each sides of the coin. Factors that ought to be do not forget embody, but aren't necessarily restrained to the subsequent:

- warmth loss / warmth gain (energy performance) thru gift constructing envelope vs. New advent code necessities

- disposal of materials from the demolition of present form

- dangerous materials likely implemented in contemporary shape (lead, asbestos, VOCs, and many others.)

- power-efficient kitchen and washing device/dryer home equipment

- green plumbing furniture (low-flow bathe heads, dual flush lavatories, and so forth.)

- the situation of the present plumbing, electric, and hvac (mechanical) structures

- the life-span of the prevailing shape vs. The life-span of a modern-day structure

- strength that might be stored over the subsequent 10, 20, 50 years with modern-day-day technology if you were to build a current home (ex: immoderate efficacy lighting fixtures; lots an awful lot less warmness loss / warm temperature gain via using manner of way of a greater green building envelope; technology together with sun PV panels, and so forth.)

It has turn out to be apparent over time that many vintage homes do no longer observe the contemporary power ratings and due to this stand as applicants for demolition. With the recommendation of your Architect or Energy Consultant, you may discover that extra money is lost yearly through electricity inefficiency and this can be stored if the whole structure have become added down and a ultra-modern-day one constructed with present day-day power green necessities in thoughts.

Chapter 4: Property Tax Liability

Property Tax Liability must be factored in to this desire as well. Adding right now to and/or transforming your contemporary home also can result in a reduced quantifiable tax base in comparison to the choice of tearing down and constructing a ultra-present day domestic. Ultimately, you'll be able to boom the price of your own home thru sporting out the remodeling undertaking accurately for this reason getting greater than what you're in all likelihood to pay in taxes.

Quantification of transforming work is generally difficult except there can be new square photos added. Unlike tearing down and building new, the re-assessment does not usually entail a whole-scale assessment with region comps. The appraised fee of a revamped home is truely resolved with the aid of the usage of set square photos estimation. Of course I propose which you verify all of this along side your close by regulating enterprise, maximum possibly the County Assessor's Office and close by Building Department. It's satisfactory to comprehend what all of the functionality implications are in advance than growing a completely last choice, because of the fact you otherwise will not have the overall photo of standard charge implications.

Understanding tax adjustments primarily based completely totally on "tear down and collect new" responsibilities

Tearing down and building a today's residence is identical to the acquisition of a modern home most effective besides that your land value does not change. With this in mind, it's far well well really worth noting that your assessed fee is determined by way of topics, particularly the land and the "upgrades" (the shape). Once you're finished with the present day advent, the honest marketplace price evaluation of the following upgrades may be finished thru doing a "stroll through" or with the aid of the usage of the assessor's evaluation of neighboring comps. You more tax burden can be decided through getting the distinction a number of the value introduced for your new house minus the evaluated really worth of the vintage home that you demolished.

It is consequently clean that in advance than embarking to your challenge, the problem of taxation will need to be considered carefully due to the truth every manner the following paintings could have some long time effect for your price range. The timing of your "tear down and assemble new residence" challenge is likewise essential as this may moreover will let you efficaciously take gain of the lowest property taxes.

What consequences does domestic addition and remodeling have on your taxes?

When it entails taxation, addition and reworking duties typically have a bonus over tearing down and beginning from scratch. This is because of the truth those varieties of tasks are subjected to a minimal tax revision and therefore you could do the paintings and decorate the fee of your own home without usually growing the tax burden with the resource of manner of a massive margin. The tax revision will broadly speakme be primarily based to your creation permit valuation and the more space you're allowed to create. It want to be referred to that now not all home enhancements are mission to a tax boom and therefore you should not fear or shrink back from home improvement for worry of tax increase.

How you may be capable of lower taxation

As a residence proprietor, you may advantage financially via tax deductibles, and therefore that is some thing you ought to truly detail in whilst selecting the manner you'd like to enhance your home. For example, in remodeling or together with without delay to your private home, one of the techniques to take gain of presidency offerings is with the resource of manner of enhancing your private home's strength normal overall performance for this reason qualifying for tremendous tax reductions. Talk on your Accountant to talk approximately all options, and a way to top notch qualify for income tax consolation, which may additionally ultimately pass an extended manner in decreasing the rate of your ordinary assignment.

To begin with, you may want to make full rate for all of the labor and materials used before filing for tax credit rating. You will however must wait until the calendar three hundred and sixty five days involves an give up in advance than filing for tax credit. You can get your tax credit rating estimates earlier than submitting for the profits tax refund but with proper recommendation from your accountant, it is able to be feasible to get massive returns thru using qualifying substances and making your property extra energy efficient. This way thinking about subjects collectively with:

- Addition of latest (wall, roof, and ground) insulation

- Installation of recent power green doorways and home domestic home windows

Chapter 5: The Benefits of an Addition or Remodel

Adding to and/or transforming a domestic is typically notion to be the exceptional and cheapest route, and in some cases, this may be actual. The secret's in know-how whether or not or now not the house you're remodeling is certainly well well worth the prices and whether or not the blessings are long term and substantial enough to warrant the efforts.

If the residence's shape is in pretty appropriate circumstance and the muse, roof, and partitions are although robust and robust, and if the structures and finishes were maintained properly through the years, then there is probably no need to rip it down. A thorough inspection should be performed all through the machine of decision-making through a certified engineer and constructing inspector to set up the modern-day-day-

day scenario. Also, your Architect let you decide out whether or no longer the changes you want finished to the shape should have any negative outcomes because of this endangering the occupants at the identical time as decreasing its lifespan.

Some reworking jobs might not require a huge rate variety and are a count number of in reality updating or touching up, whilst others require massive labor that might require masses of coins in the gadget. One of the best advantages with which encompass directly to or reworking your home is that you are more likely at the manner to carry out the venture in tiers depending on your economic competencies. This therefore method you will be able to address a unmarried part of the residence, giving it diligent interest earlier than embarking on some other component of the home. For instance, in case you intend to increase the gap of your residing room and expand one of the bedrooms to offer you with a major bedroom, it is straightforward to start with one a part of the task. Once you are via, you'll be able to embark on the other aspect with out constantly vacating the whole residence and residing in a hotel. With a professional Architect running for your mission, it is going to be a lot less hard to acquire first-class effects inside a brief term on the identical time as being capable of do the work in degrees till the entirety is finished.

Adding onto and reworking your property can probable let you introduce contemporary and updated touches to your house often with out feeling the functionality monetary pressure this is every now and then related to new homes. Compared to ripping down and building new, the method of transforming and such as on your modern domestic can frequently revel in much less draining or stressful, due to the fact the quantity of the scope appears lots extra plausible.

In addition, permits for reworking and together with a room or functions to your property frequently come at a much lower price in comparison to that of tearing down and constructing new. Remodeling and which include to the residence moreover permits you to maintain the statistics and the man or woman of the older structure, particularly if you decide to keep something particular capabilities may also exist. If you're making plans to resell the older domestic, doing some number one remodeling, or including splendid functions or growing it is able to appreciably boom its price sooner or later permitting you to make extra money out of the sale in area of going to the problem of constructing a brand new house. Or in case you don't plan to transport out and sell, you may simply decide to convert or add on in choice to constructing new because of a robust an emotional attachment you could need to your house.

If your house has been in lifestyles for decades, has any ancient fee or historical man or woman, and has been maintained well, you could discover that the awesome detail to do is to transform and add some factor enhancements you preference. Just make certain to pick out your dreams on the get-flow a very good manner to ensure you don't lose sight of the specific motive. Professional advice can be very vital on the equal time as thinking about this kind of undertaking, and also you'll want to artwork carefully collectively together with your Architect and in all likelihood numerous distinctive experts (structural, mechanical, power, MEP, and so on.) to look at the antique residence to determine whether or no longer it is able to accommodate desired additions and upgrades while at the equal time adhering to your network building codes and hints.

It is likewise essential to endure in thoughts the area of your vintage house in advance than you decide to rip it down and assemble a present day one. There are conditions even as logistics ought to reveal this sort of project to be improper and luxurious specifically if the antique residence is placed in a place wherein accessibility is a undertaking. For example, in case your vintage residence is surrounded by means of different houses or functions that could make it tough to put off the vintage building substances and produce in new ones, then you could probably want to have shifting device or tool to help do this kind of paintings. The impact of this is that you can become incurring extra expenses for this particular paintings even in advance than you may start constructing the modern-day shape.

One closing interest with reference to this desire is that you may need to check along side your close by constructing branch to ensure your own home isn't in a historical district or region that could have first rate regulations as to the compatibility of architectural fashion. If you are required to preserve any positive historic skills, or positioned up snap shots of your proposed project to a Historic Board for his or her assessment and approval, this is really some problem you've idea thru and surely researched in advance.

Chapter 6: The Benefits of Tearing Down and Building New

Despite the tone of the preceding economic catastrophe, of direction there may be motives why tearing down and building new might be more first-rate.

First, it's pretty viable that your present domestic certainly doesn't offer all which you desire, in phrases of capability or architectural format. Your dreams aren't being met, and it would take some of paintings to adjust your private home to get what you're seeking to benefit. This is particularly actual for individuals who need to shop for antique houses in up and coming (or already up and walking) neighborhoods in which residential land has come to be scarce, unavailable, and high-priced. In this form of scenario, seeking out an antique residence, tearing it down and building a contemporary one may also virtually be the most prudent path of movement, specially if you have the financial capability to do it. And once more to the concept of Return on Investment (ROI), you may find out that normally, tearing down and constructing new will be triumphant. New construction offers you a clean slate from which you may assemble a domestic that sincerely meets your dreams and aspirations.

With modern-day building technology, tearing down and building new allows owners to take gain of nowadays's more electricity-green homes and modern aesthetics which reflect on our current day way of life and dreams. A new home frees you from bulky layout limitations which might be related to the approach of modifications with the resource of way of additions and reworking. You will extra often than no longer be amazed to find out that tearing down and constructing new is truely a lot much less high priced than assignment a large scale addition or renovation project.

If your gift residence is structurally now not worth, or if the thoughts you have got in mind for modifications comprise along with on a second tale, the probably maximum feasible choice to pursue is that of tearing down and starting from scratch. Your architect or a structural engineer will can help you determine whether or not your vintage residence is structurally match to help you with this selection. Tearing down the prevailing domestic to construct a trendy one from scratch comes with vital architectural blessings that encompass first-class and inexperienced heating and cooling, nicely designed living vicinity that caters on your specific desires and modern aesthetics.

How tearing down and building new works

First of all, you'll want to choose out your exceptional layout in advance than embarking on a tear down and rebuild task. This shape of a layout desire should reflect your charge range, scope, software program application, aesthetic alternatives, and you will be great off working with an Architect who can present to you several options from which to select the abilities which you similar to the most.

Your Architect will need to go to the website in which the vintage house stands, studies the code requirements, art work with you to increase a software program, after which provide you with severa layout answers to study and talk with you. Then, your Architect will post the drawings to the local regulatory businesses for approvals in advance than you can be issued a permit. During the identical equipped length time body that the constructing department is reviewing the drawings, your Architect assist you to in the bidding and negotiations section wherein you solicit proposals for production from severa special elegant contractors. By the time the building department concludes their have a look at and permits had been issued, you'll be ready to lease the contractor to begin the method of demolition and waste disposal (or recycling). Next, the website may be cleared and the brand new shape can be constructed.

Chapter 7: How to Patch a Hole in Your Wall

I: Tools and substances you may need

II: Small punctures, gouges, nail holes

Small punctures, gouges, nail holes, and dents inclusive of those made through the use of manner of nails, screws, screw drivers, molly screws, and lots of others. Are the only and simplest harm for your partitions to restore. Although those forms of damage are just like repair, the strategies range barely, so we will cowl every kind of harm one at a time to offer you an intensive expertise of a manner to repair the specific form of damage you could have.

Small punctures and nail holes

For the ones sorts of damage you can want a small amount of spackling paste and a small trowel or putty knife. If you do no longer already have these items, they may be supplied out of your community hardware or paint shops.

It's constantly an remarkable idea at the same time as patching holes for your partitions, to transport any furniture properly out of the way so you may not get any of the patching fabric on it.

You want to also placed a drop cloth at the ground to protect your wood, tile, linoleum, or carpeted floor. After transferring any furniture out of the way, lay out the drop material right away below the broken vicinity of the wall. Secure the drop material to the wall with masking tape. This will prevent the drop fabric from transferring out of feature. Next, for super effects, you have to thoroughly wash the wall to do away with any dirt or grease that would save you accurate adhesion for the spackling paste or paint you can use later. Then, get rid of any sticking out cloth from round the rims of the hollow, (paint, drywall, and so forth.) with the brink of the putty knife or trowel the usage of a scraping movement. This is wonderful achieved thru shielding your putty knife or trowel at about a 30-diploma mind-set in the direction of the wall and drawing it across the hole in the direction of you. Never push it faraway from you. You can also turn out to be turning your little hollow proper right right into a massive gouge. After this is completed and the wall around the hole is easy and flush, take a small quantity spackling paste from its container with the stop of the putty knife or difficulty of the trowel. Press it in to the hole retaining the putty knife or trowel as flat toward the wall as viable. Then easy it out and put off any greater spackling paste with the same scraping method as you used earlier to get rid of any protrusions. When the spackling paste is dry (this takes just a few minutes) the wall is ready so that you can examine the paint.

If your wall has numerous nail holes in it, they'll all want to be patched within the equal manner. In this situation, you could most probable should repaint the entire wall.

In most instances, because of age or discoloration of the prevailing paint on the wall, the whole wall can also moreover need to be repainted. In the case that the prevailing paint is reasonably new, you can no longer need to color the whole wall. The pleasant way to check this is to identify paint the patched place best and permit the paint dry. If the brand new paint fits the antique paint cautiously enough in your desires, then you may no longer want to paint the entire wall. However, if it does no longer healthy, you will want to shade the complete wall. For centered commands on portray your walls, consult with segment IV, "Finishing the venture with a extremely-cutting-edge coat of paint".

Gouges and dents

Gouges and dents that do not penetrate definitely via the drywall are almost as easy to patch as small punctures and nail holes. In the case of gouges, most will need to have the torn or peeled paint and drywall across the gouge trimmed away to clean the edges for patching. This may be accomplished with a pointy hobby knife or razor blade. In some times, it is able to be scraped away within the same manner as described earlier inside the section on small punctures and nail holes. Also as with small punctures and nail holes, the wall should be thoroughly washed to prepare the surface for patching. When this is finished, blend a small amount of patching plaster or plaster of Paris (both will paintings high-quality) constant with the aggregate instructions at the package.

Make sure that the plaster you may be the use of is glowing and now not starting to form tough lumps in it. This will cause the patch to be susceptible and disintegrate effortlessly. Mix simplest as loads as you can want to patch your gouge or dent. Let the aggregate stand for a brief on the equal time as to thicken constantly checking the consistency. When the mixture reaches a thick pasty consistency, it is prepared to be applied to the wall. If you try to apply it to the wall in advance than it reaches this consistency it will run out of your gouge or dent and make your interest a good deal harder than crucial.

Just earlier than you exercise the plaster, you want to wet the area with simple cool water in a twig bottle to make the software method flow smoother. The dry plaster within the wall will in any other case draw the moisture out of the patching plaster too short and prevent particular adhesion to the gouge or dent.

As quickly as you moist the location, speedy take a look at the plaster to the wall smoothing it into the dent or gouge. You ought to artwork fast at this element because of the fact the plaster dries brief. If it receives too thick earlier than you exercising it, it will be nearly not possible to apply and couldn't adhere to the wall very well. If this takes vicinity you may need to discard this batch of plaster and mix up some other batch. After you easy the plaster into the gouge or dent, look ahead to any sagging of the plaster. If you spot the plaster beginning to sag, clean it out with the trowel using an upward motion. Repeat this as regularly as vital till the plaster has hardened sufficient no longer to sag.

When the plaster is really dry and bloodless to the touch, it is geared up to be sanded clean. Use medium grit sandpaper within the starting to smooth out the roughest quantities of the plaster. Then, use best grit sandpaper to smooth and blend the rims of the patch with the wall. Remember plaster is a particularly clean and powdery material that sands very with out hassle, so it's miles very vital which you strive no longer to position an excessive amount of strain on the sandpaper at the identical time as sanding it. After you've finished with the sanding, the equal manner as turn out to be defined in "Small punctures and nail holes", you are organized to begin repainting. For sure instructions on repainting your wall (or walls), talk over with phase IV, "completing the undertaking with a brand new coat of paint".

III: Doorknob and Other Medium Sized Holes

Medium sized holes that penetrate certainly thru the drywall might require a slightly more complicated approach to patching them. Because in their size it's miles extra hard to get the plaster to live placed inside the hole till it's miles dry, in particular within the case of a hole non-insulated wall. To preserve the plaster from falling into or out of the wall on the identical time as utilising the plaster patch, it's miles going to be crucial to provide the hole with a backing to maintain the plaster in area until it hardens. This is completed by manner of rolling up some newspaper to the approximate period of the hollow, then twisting it to make it pretty "spring like". Then the twisted newspaper is stuffed into the hole just so it presses in competition to the other thing of the wall and holds itself in competition to the again of the hole you are patching. In the case of an insulated wall, the insulation itself will offer most of the backing crucial. In this case, you can first-class want to position a flat layer of newspaper maximum of the wall and the insulation. Make it thick sufficient to maintain itself tightly closer to the decrease lower back of the hollow and prevent the moisture of the patching plaster from being absorbed into the insulation.

Before you start, make sure to position out a drop cloth at the ground under the hollow and solid it to the wall with protecting tape. This will defend the ground and make clean-up less difficult.

After stuffing the newspaper backing into the hole, trim away any unfastened plaster, paint, or drywall paper that may be round the edges of the hollow through decreasing and sanding. If there are any ragged quantities of drywall paper spherical the rims of the hole, they can be trimmed away with a sharp interest knife or razor blade. Loose paint and plaster may be sanded off. Then wash the wall to remove any dirt, grease, or loose dust from sanding.

When you're finished making ready the hole to be patched, mix enough plaster to fill the hollow in line with the commands at the plaster package deal. Then allow the aggregate stand, checking it frequently till it's miles thick and pasty. Then moist the edges of the hollow to be patched just earlier than applying the plaster to the hollow. This is to insure a first-rate bond and prevent the dry plaster within the wall from drawing the moisture out of the patching plaster to brief. Now follow the plaster to the hollow using a medium sized trowel. This is nice performed by means of the usage of scooping a beneficiant amount of plaster out of the integration container with the cease of the trowel, then pushing it lightly into the hole with an upward motion. Continue to do that till the hollow is definitely stuffed. The plaster will tend to sag a piece, however don't fear, just hold to clean the plaster out with an upward motion of the trowel.

If the plaster starts to crack and cut up while you're doing this, spray a hint water on it with the spray bottle and smooth it out with the trowel till it's miles employer enough now not to sag. Then permit it dry till it is cold to touch. Sometimes in massive holes the plaster also can reduce lower back a little as it dries. If this takes area it usually leaves an indentation in the patch and you can need to use a second coat of plaster. Mix enough plaster to fill the indentation. Wet the patch first and then study the plaster to the patch. Then easy it out with the trowel as you did before with an upward movement. Let the patch dry very well.

When the patch is dry, sand it easy, first with medium grit sandpaper to take off the tough spots and any excess plaster. Then sand it smooth with the super grit sandpaper to aggregate the edges with the wall. When the seams among the wall and patch are blended together simply so they can't be seen or felt, you are prepared for the final step, painting the wall.

IV: Large Holes

Large holes require a completely remarkable method to patching than small or medium sized holes do. If the hole is extra than three" or 4" in diameter, it can now not be possible to patch it definitely the usage of newspaper to lower back the hole and fill it with plaster as you may with the smaller medium sized holes. Generally, if the hole is bigger than 3" or four" in diameter it's going to nearly be not possible to get the newspaper to stay in area with out it falling down within the wall. This can occasionally be difficult even within the medium sized holes.

What you will want to do in this case is to patch the hole with a scrap piece of drywall of the same thickness as the drywall to your wall. To do that, you can first need to diploma the thickness of the drywall for your wall, if you don't already realize what the thickness of it is. Before you could measure the thickness as it should be, you should make a smooth aspect to diploma. See example three-1. This is crucial because of the fact, in maximum instances when the drywall is broken in this way, the rims of the drywall across the hole typically normally tend to unfold out a bit.

First, lay out a drop fabric on the ground beneath the hole to be patched and stable it to the wall with protective tape.

Using a sharp software software knife or extremely good tooth discovered blade, lessen away the ragged issue at the lowest of the hollow. Then, the usage of a ruler or tape diploma, degree the thickness of the drywall on the factor you cut away. If you have not any scrap drywall laying around your property or storage, as maximum people do no longer, then you may visit a domestic improvement save or lumber outdoor and purchase a piece of drywall the thickness you need. Before you skip buy your drywall, you'll need to recognize the size of the piece you will need.

To find out what length (width and top) scrap of drywall you can need, you want to first put together the hole for patching. The following paragraphs provide an motive at the back of the tactics for making organized the hollow and using the patch.

Preparation

To put together the hole, you can must lessen it out huge in a square shape. First, you may want to find the studs on both aspect of the hole. You can do this in several techniques. The most effective manner is to use an virtual stud finder. It works via detecting the metal nails or screws used to fasten the drywall to the studs. If you do no longer have a stud finder, you may use a strong magnet to discover the nails or screws.

Another way, if you have an tremendous ear, is to softly tap on the wall with a hammer transferring across the wall as you tap time and again. The sound it makes will trade slightly in pitch. For example, within the bays the various studs the sound might be a decrease pitched hole sound. On the studs, the sound could be a slightly better pitched extra strong sound. Another way is if there is an outlet or transfer close to the hole (a great deal much less than sixteen") there might be a stud on one side or the alternative due to the fact the mounting bins that the switches or stores are installed in are installation on the studs.

The final manner, if the hole is large sufficient, is to obtain in with a ruler or measuring tape and extend it to at the least one facet of the hole till it hits a stud and word the dimensions. Then transfer the dimension to the out of doors of the wall and make a mark wherein the stud is placed. Then repeat this system for the alternative component of the hole. See example 3-2 on net web page 9. When the use of this approach, be very cautious now not to drop your ruler or measuring tape or you may lose it in the wall.

Once you've got got located and marked wherein the studs are on each issue of the hole, degree from the ground to the very excellent point of the hole. Make positive to preserve the tape degree right away up and right all the manner all the way down to get the most accurate period. Then upload 1" to this length and make a mark at the wall at the stud places on each facet of the hole. Using a proper away facet, draw a line among those marks with a pencil. Next, degree from the road you definitely drew to the bottom issue of the hollow. Add 1" to this size and make a mark at every stud places from the street above the hole. Draw a line among the ones marks. This will shape the top and backside borders of the patch hole. Connect those two strains together at the stud locations with vertical strains forming a rectangle. (See the instance)

Make nice that the traces are straight and the corners are rectangular (at 90-degree angles).This will assist to insure that the patch will wholesome nicely into the hole. Now lessen the drywall out along the strains carefully with a software knife or observed and take away the drywall from the hole. When this is executed, trim up and smooth the top and backside edges of the hole. The aspect edges have now been cut flush with the studs and need to be trimmed lower again ¾" to as a minimum one" greater to expose enough of the stud to nail the patch to it. Draw a vertical line parallel to the aspect edges of the hole ¾" to as a minimum one" from the edge of the hollow. Carefully reduce on the traces with the utility knife and put off the strips of drywall to expose the studs. If there are any nails or screws exposed by way of the use of this way, do away with them. Now trim up and easy the thing edges of the hole ensuring they're immediately and the corners are nevertheless rectangular. Now you can degree the width and top of the hollow for the patch.

Applying the patch

Now which you have the measurements for the patch, you are prepared to buy the drywall on your patch. Make effective you get a piece of drywall large than you need so you'll have room for trimming and shaping it to healthful. Also make sure it's far huge sufficient to lessen a 2nd patch in case of mistakes. If your hole isn't too huge, you'll be capable of find a scrap piece of drywall at the shop. Some shops will supply away the ones scraps free of rate.

Cut the piece of drywall to the measurements you took from the hole. Make positive you cut it to in form pretty tightly inside the hole. This will make filling the seams much less difficult and you can not must use as lots plaster or spackling paste to fill the seam gaps. Once you have got the patch lessen to healthy, area it in the hole and nail it in place with drywall nails. The fashion of nails you could want will depend upon how huge your patch is. Put a nail in each nook and a nail every 3" to 4" apart on every elements.

When you nail it in location, mindset the nails barely inside the course of the studs so they will preserve more potent, but ensure not to perspective the nails too much or the heads will tear and spoil the edges. See example under. Be cautious when nailing it in vicinity so that you may not emerge as with each other hole to patch. When the nail heads are flush with the ground of the drywall, tap them in most effective a little extra to shape a slight dimple within the drywall patch. This is, (correctly sufficient) called dimpling. This is finished so the dimple may be complete of plaster to cover the nail heads. After that is performed, you are organized to mix the patching plaster to fill the seams and dimples. Mix a small amount of plaster consistent with the commands at the plaster bundle deal deal.

Mix the plaster till it has a medium thick soupy consistency. Spray some cool water over the vicinity with a sprig bottle after which trowel the plaster into the seams and dimples till they will be filled to a mild mound over them. Let the plaster dry thoroughly. Then the usage of medium grit sandpaper, sand the seams flush with the wall and patch. Then sand the seams clean with the first rate grit sandpaper. Be careful now not to sand an excessive amount of. If you do, you could sand the plaster out of the dimples. Next, test to make sure there are not any gaps within the seams. If you discover any gaps or air bubbles seen within the seams or dimples, they'll be full of spackling paste within the identical manner as described in segment I. When that is completed, you are organized to repaint your wall. Refer to section IV, for focused instructions on portray your partitions.

V: Finishing the Job with a New Coat of Paint

Now that you've finished patching your wall, it is time to place a present day coat of paint in your wall. Unless you're making plans to color the complete room a extraordinary colour than it's miles proper now, you'll need to get paint that cautiously fits the antique paint. Even then, it's going to now not in shape perfectly with the vintage paint. For example, say that you painted your residing room a few months within the beyond and you still have a number of the paint that you used left over. You need to identify paint over a patched hollow on one of the walls.

The left over paint will not healthy the antique paint on the wall flawlessly because of age and discoloration of the vintage paint. You'll be able to see a distinction a number of the antique and new paint. For this cause, it's miles recommended that you paint the entire wall as opposed to spot painting over the patches exceptional. If the vintage paint is truely too badly discolored and the difference a number of the freshly painted wall and the vintage paint on the opportunity partitions is certainly too apparent, then it can be crucial to repaint the entire room. Of course, the choice is yours whether or no longer or not to perceive paint, paint the whole wall, or paint the entire room, depending at the state of affairs of the partitions and paint and how formidable you are. For the nice possible results, the writer strongly recommends portray the entire room. For this purpose, the rest of this phase will deliver interest to the techniques for portray the entire room. However, the ones methods may be tailor-made for portray really one wall as nicely.

Preparations

The first element you may need to do is pass the furnishings out of the way to allow numerous ft of place among it and the walls. It's exceptional to transport all the fixtures out of the room you need to color. This will allow you the most room to art work. If it's no longer possible or practical that allows you to waft it out of the room, then you can float all of it into the middle of the room and cowl it with plastic drop cloths. These are to be had in most home improvement and paint shops in plenty of sizes and are priced very pretty. The next element you could need to do is to unfold drop cloths at the floor and stable them to the bottom of the baseboards with shielding tape if the floor is protected with carpet.

If the floor defensive is wood, tile, or linoleum, you could tape the drop cloth immediately to the floor up within the course of the baseboards. If your baseboards are non-painted surfaces, you can tape the drop cloths to the top edge of the baseboards ensuring the baseboards are absolutely covered. When taping the drop cloths the tape have to continually be performed alongside the brink of the drop material in location of all through it. See example underneath.

Next, masks each other unpainted surfaces the use of shielding tape and newspaper. When covering, make sure that the tape is freed from wrinkles or bubbles and firmly pressed down or paint will seep beneath it.

After the masking is completed, take away all the wall plates. These are the covers over the stores and switches hung on through screws. As you remove the wall plates, screw the screws lower lower back inside the switches and shops just so they'll not wander away. Now you'll need to clean off ant dust or grease that can be on the walls. Stains that might not wash off will want to be treated with a stain killer/primer or they will bleed via the paint and smash your paint system.

Painting

Now that the preparations are complete you are organized to start painting your partitions. First, you'll need to do the trim art work. For this you'll need to apply a broom (preferably a 3" angled brush) or a 3" trim curler. The trim art work is finished, by portray carefully round all of the perimeters of the areas to be painted.

That is to say, along all of the masked edges, along the corners most of the ceilings and walls, within the corners amongst partitions, along the baseboards, across the stores and switches, and across the doors and home domestic windows. This is performed so you won't need to get to close to any of the rims with the large roller and risk messing some component up.

When you finish with the trim paintings, use a big nine" roller to color the rest of the walls. To gather the pleasant effects roll the paint on slowly in vertical strokes from floor to ceiling overlapping the strokes. Rolling the paint on slowly will help save you the curler from splattering the paint during you. Roll the roller within the paint tray each three or four strokes to replenish the roller with paint. Don't try to roll the paint on to thin. If you do, you can need to colour a second coat to cover the vintage paint completely. However, in case your walls are quite grimy, you can need a 2d coat except.

Chapter 8: How to Replace an Outlet or Switch

I: Tools and materials you may want

II: Outlet and Switch Configurations

There are numerous common configurations of shops and switches along side mixtures of both. There also are precise forms of shops and switches. It's vital so you can realise what configuration and forms of switches and stores you have got got to help you find the right alternative factors. In this segment, we are going to cover the maximum commonplace types and configurations to help you find out the kinds and configurations you may need to update or change to a extremely good configuration or type. The following is a listing of the varieties of switches, shops and configurations we are going to be masking on this segment.

Types of switches

Single toggle

Single lighted toggle

Toggle kind dimmer

Rotary type dimmer

Rocker type transfer

Types of shops

Single with 2 grounded sockets

Single with out grounded sockets

Outlet/switch aggregate

Outlet with incorporated breaker

Single w/ one by one controlled sockets

Single w/ one managed socket

Types of configurations

Single outlet

Double outlet

Single outlet with single transfer

Single outlet with double transfer

Double outlet with single switch

Double outlet with double transfer

Single outlet one after the alternative managed with double switch

Double outlet one after the opportunity controlled with double switch

Double transfer configuration

Single outlet with integrated breaker and single or double switch

First, we are able to talk the suitable configurations because of the fact they may be used to perceive the form of configuration you are interested in changing in your private home. The first of those is the unmarried outlet configuration.

Single outlet configuration

This is a famous configuration with a single outlet that has sockets to plug home tool into. The cover plate may have massive holes for the sockets and one screw hole. It'll diploma 2¾"x 4½".

Double outlet configuration

This is a commonplace configuration that includes single shops hooked up side-with the aid of the use of-component in a double mounting area. The cowl plate might also have four big holes for the sockets and screw holes. It'll be approximately 4½" square.

Single outlet with unmarried transfer

This configuration is most customarily used in kitchens, and lavatories. It combines a unmarried outlet with a unmarried transfer below a 4½" square cover plate. The plate will have a rectangular hollow centered on one facet with screw holes above and beneath it. On the alternative thing, it has two large holes for the sockets and one screw hollow in amongst them.

Single outlet with double transfer

This configuration includes a unmarried outlet set up in a double field beside a double switch. A double switch has switches in a single unit that mounts beneath the equal cowl plate as a single outlet. When established beside a single outlet, a double outlet plate might be used.

Double outlet with single switch

This configuration includes two unmarried stores and one unmarried switch hooked up in a triple field. The cover plate ought to have four massive holes for the sockets and a tough and speedy of transfer mounting holes on a triple plate. The cowl plate calls for 4 mounting screws, 2 for the switch and 1 every for the stores.

Double outlet with double transfer

This is a configuration wherein two unmarried outlets are mixed with a double switch set up in a triple field. The cover plate can also have three devices of single outlet mounting holes or six oval socket holes with 3 screw mounting holes.

Single outlet one at a time controlled with double transfer

This configuration will to begin with appearance similar to the single outlet with double switch configuration. To discover if that is the case, take a look at each socket with the useful resource of plugging in a lamp and turning on one or the alternative transfer. If the lamp is going on and stale with both of the switches, and the alternative socket is one after the other managed with the aid of the opposite switch, then that is the case.

Double outlet separately controlled with double transfer

In this configuration, the double switch will manage every of the two unmarried shops one after the other. One transfer controls sockets and the opportunity switch controls the alternative sockets.

Double switch configuration

This is a easy configuration wherein two unmarried switches are installation facet-by-issue in a double box with a double switch cover plate.

Single outlet with incorporated breaker and unmarried or double transfer

In this configuration a unmarried outlet is controlled and protected by means of a covered breaker. The breaker trips and turns off the outlet if an overload takes place. Sometimes the ones breaker controlled shops are set up alongside difficulty a single or double transfer. These configurations are generally positioned in bathrooms. The switches can also manipulate lighting fixtures for mirrors or for room lighting fixtures. The breaker prepared outlet, might be used for hair dryers, electric powered powered toothbrushes, and so on.

If a breaker organized outlet is set up on my own, the cover plate could be a unmarried length plate with a massive square hole about 2½"x 1¼" within the center and the mounting screw holes at pinnacle and bottom. If the opening is installed with a unmarried switch, the plate may have the identical antique switch holes in addition to the breaker outlet hollow. If it's far set up with a double switch, then there can be a difficult and rapid of single outlet holes in location of the unmarried switch holes.

These, are the maximum commonplace (and a few not so common) configurations you are in all likelihood to stumble upon in your home or condominium. As you may see by using their descriptions, some of the right varieties of cowl plates are interchangeable with specific configurations. This may be to be had in some times at the same time as you want to alternate the configuration. You may not need to replace the triumphing cowl plate if what you are converting it to will healthy the holes inside the cover plate.

In this subsequent segment, we are going to describe exceptional types of switches maximum typically used within the home. They are to be had pretty a big type of types and styles. However, we are going to only be discussing some of them. The ones you'll maximum probably have in your property.

Single toggle

This is a unmarried switch with a lever type address. Some of these switches can have screws on the edges for connecting the wires to it. Some might also have wires popping out of them called "pigtails" and can be related to the wires inside the box with twine nuts.

Single lighted toggle

This transfer is just like the formerly cited transfer except the toggle cope with is lighted. In this transfer, the lighted toggle cope with is off at the same time as the switch is grew to turn out to be to the "on" function. When the switch is inside the "off" role the deal with lighting up so it could be seen in the dark.

Toggle type dimmer

This sort of switch usually has the "pigtail" wires coming out of the lower lower back of it. It can also have either a lighted deal with or an unlighted one. This form of switch is used to dim a light within the room. The switch has variable settings the various "off" and "on" positions to dim the mild to numerous levels using a variable resistance circuit or a rheostat.

Rotary kind dimmer

This sort of dimmer switch has a dial or knob kind deal with. This dimmer turns in a rotary way rather than the lever type up and down movement of the toggle transfer, however plays the identical function of dimming a mild as the toggle type dimmer.

Rocker switches

These switches are extra low profile than the toggle switches with a extensive "v" shape. This shape is designed to rock up and down at the same time as the pinnacle or backside edges of the "v" are pressed. They come with lighted or unlighted handles also. The cover plate that fits this form of switch is the most effective with the massive rectangular hole inside the middle.

Last, but now not least, this section covers the excellent types of shops that you could discover in your own home. Most of those have internal variations, but some variety in most effective the way they're installation. This is probably covered in greater element later in the ones descriptions.

Single outlet with grounded sockets

This outlet is a unmarried outlet with , three prong sockets in a single unit. The 1/three prong is for grounding something that is plugged into it. Most stores these days are grounded and more domestic device are made with the 1/3 ground prong on their plugs. This allows defend the gadget from being damaged through manner of strength surges.

Single outlet with out ground

These are generally older stores which have not been changed for the purpose that grounded shops came into use. However, ungrounded shops are despite the truth that available if you want to replace one and do not need to update it with a grounded outlet. Adapters are available must you want to plug a grounded system into an ungrounded outlet.

NOTE: As with ungrounded shops, these adapters don't provide good enough safety in competition to power surges or spikes and the author recommends that each one ungrounded shops be replaced with grounded shops.

Outlet/transfer combo

In this combination unit, one of the outlet sockets is modified with a transfer much like those utilized in a double transfer. In this unit, the transfer typically controls the socket. However, it could be with out problem altered to manipulate some issue else with the aid of disposing of a metallic connecting tab that connects the switch to the socket.

Outlet with blanketed breaker

As in quick defined earlier, the ones shops have breakers built into them to protect the sockets and domestic system associated with them from harm because of overloads or electricity surges. They are maximum commonly utilized in toilets to be used with hair dryers, electric powered powered powered toothbrushes and shavers.

Single outlet w/ one by one controlled sockets

These stores are similar to the single stores besides that the metallic connecting tabs have been eliminated to permit each socket to be related to separate switches for person control of the sockets.

Single outlet with one managed socket

This outlet is just like the previous one except most effective one of the sockets is managed via manner of way of a transfer. The unique socket is burdened right now to the power and isn't controlled.

Now you are more acquainted with the different types and configurations of the switches and stores most typically discovered in houses and residences nowadays. You want as a manner to with out trouble apprehend the types and configurations which can be of specific interest to you and your needs.

In the following section, we are going to talk a way to eliminate an vintage damaged or unwanted outlet. We'll moreover discuss a few safety pointers to which you want to pay close interest. They want to store your existence.

III: Removing the Old Outlet

To remove an old outlet, the number one aspect you could want to do is, check all of the safety hints, particularly safety tip, number one.

Safety tip #1 is to ensure the energy to the circuit containing the outlet you need to replace is have become off. It's in no way an tremendous concept to try to art work on an electrical device of any type with the energy grew to emerge as on. It can't be burdened strongly enough, the significance of gazing all of these safety pointers. So, please ensure you study all of them and be secure.

Safety tip quantity , is to make certain you try this opportunity procedure throughout the daytime. You do not want to be fumbling round within the darkish looking to replace an outlet with the electricity have become off.

Safety tip wide range three, is to make certain the gear you operate have insulated handles. Though the electricity is grew to emerge as off, this'll assist prevent electric powered shocks within the occasion the incorrect breaker changed into grew to become off.

Safety tip sizable variety 4 is to ensure you in no manner touch more than one wire at a time. Even with the electricity grew to become off, it's far better to be secure than sorry.

To flip off the circuit, discover the fuse, or breaker area in your house or apartment. If you realise which fuse or breaker controls the circuit containing the outlet to get replaced, turn it off. If you do not know which one it's miles, then you could have to check the circuits to discover. We can assume then, that your fuse or breaker panel isn't always classified. If this is the case, then this is the right time to label it for destiny reference.

Before you begin checking out the circuits, make certain a lamp, or TV, or radio, or some aspect is grew to end up on in each room so you will be able to inform what circuit you're sorting out.

If the hollow you're converting, although works, plug some detail into it, and turn it on. This way you could make certain it's miles off whilst you turn off the circuit to that room, because from time to time some rooms have a couple of circuit. Then move once more to the fuse or breaker panel and flip off the number one circuit. Then, go searching and notice what modified into turned off. When you find out what have become grew to become off via the usage of the primary circuit you're attempting out, bypass decrease lower back to the fuse or breaker panel and label it. Repeat this approach for every circuit in the fuse or breaker discipline till you've got got they all categorised.

By this time, you may have determined the circuit that controls the hollow you are changing. Turn this circuit off and depart the others on. Now you may flip off all of the belongings you grew to grow to be on to test the circuits.

Now which you've found and have become off the circuit that controls the hollow you want to update, you are equipped to start getting rid of the vintage outlet. First, unplug a few detail that may be plugged into it. Next, you can need to dispose of the cover plate over the opening. This is finished through manner of casting off the screw in the middle of the plate maximum of the two sockets. Then you may remove the quilt plate. Once the duvet plate is out of the manner, you may see the entire outlet unit. You'll see the steel mounting brackets at the pinnacle and bottom of the unit, and the mounting screws that preserve the hole in place in the mounting discipline. Remove those mounting screws. Now, slowly pull the hole right away out of the sector being cautious of the wires so you do now not harm them off. When the hole is pulled out, you will be capable of see how the wires are connected to it.

There are methods that the wires can be related to the outlet. One way is with screws on each aspect of the hole. If this is the case, in reality loosen the screws and remove the wires preserving the wires apart and at the same element because it modified into removed. This is important as maximum new stores are polarized.

The specific way the wires can be related is with the stripped forestall of the wires being inserted into holes in the once more of the opening. In this case, there is probably slots next to the holes. These slots are for releasing the wires. (See instance). Insert a narrow, flat blade screwdriver into the slots to launch the wires. If the wires do now not release, you can lessen the wires off near the outlet and strip the insulation off approximately ½" lower returned from the cease.

Now the outlet must be removed and you will be prepared to position within the cutting-edge outlet.

IV: Installing the New Outlet

To installation the modern-day outlet, you have picks. Most new shops have techniques to connect the wires. The first is with the aid of the usage of the screws supplied on the edges of the hollow. The distinct is thru placing the wires into holes furnished in the decrease lower back of the opening. The simplest manner to attach the wires to the hole can be to connect it the equal manner the antique outlet have become associated. However, in case you'd like to attach it otherwise in your comfort, you can reap this pretty effects. If your vintage outlet grow to be related using the screws, your wires can also have curved leads to which they were wrapped across the screws. If you want to attach the modern outlet the usage of the holes in region of the screws, you may want to straighten out the ends of the wires with more than one pliers.

Then honestly insert the wires into the holes. Make first-rate to insert every cord into the hole closest to the screw it became related to at the antique outlet.

Also, make sure the hollow is proper aspect up. Right issue up is with the rounded grounding holes in the direction of the lowest of the hole. If your outlet is an ungrounded type, there need to be a marking on the mounting bracket indicating "top" to show how it's miles to be established. Insert the wires into the holes as a long way as they may go. If any naked wire nevertheless indicates out of doors of the hollow, then you definitely surely ought to eliminate the cord and reduce off as an lousy lot as emerge as displaying outdoor of the hollow. To insure against any short circuits it's far exceptional that the insulation of the cord goes all of the manner as masses because the case of the hollow. Then reinsert the wire into the hole. Do the equal with the other twine.

NOTE: On most new stores there may be an indentation in the issue of the opening case labeled due to the fact the wire strip manual. Lay the twine within the indentation with the insulation touching the outlet case. Then reduce the twine the period of the indentation. The cord will then be the right length to insert in the holes.

If the antique outlet turned into connected the usage of the holes, and you'd as an alternative use the screws, then make sure the wires are stripped lower back far enough to permit the bare ends of the wires to wrap all through the screws. Then the use of a pair of needle nostril pliers, bend the naked ends of the wires into a semi-round arc or hook shape and be part of the wires to the screws. Once the wires are attached to the hole, lightly push the outlet and wires lower decrease again into the mounting box. Then insert the 2 mounting screws thru the opening's mounting bracket and into the mounting holes within the mounting place. Tighten the screws making sure the hollow is targeted within the field. Then update the cover plate over the opening and solid it in area with its mounting screw and the challenge is finished.

V: Replacing the Old Switch

Just as described in phase III, "getting rid of the antique outlet", you need to have a examine the protection tips and make certain the energy to the circuit containing the switch to get replaced is became off. After the circuit is turned off, unscrew the 2 screws on the quilt plate and get rid of the cover plate. Next, unscrew the switch mounting screws at the pinnacle and backside of the mounting bracket. Now gently pull the transfer proper away out of the mounting discipline. Just as with the stores, the wires to the transfer can be connected via screws or inserted into holes in the lower back of the transfer.

If the wires are inserted in the holes inside the once more of the switch, there can be slots subsequent to the holes to launch the wires. Insert the pinnacle of a narrow, flat blade screwdriver into the slots to launch the wires. If the wires might not launch, reduce them off subsequent to the opening and strip the insulation once more about ½" from the surrender. If the wires are linked to the switch with screws, loosen the screws and dispose of the wires from the switch. Make certain to keep the wires aside and on the equal factor as they were removed. If the screws the wires were connected to are each on the same factor of the switch, hold them inside the relative positions that they've been in whilst associated with the transfer. Now that the vintage switch has been eliminated from the mounting field, you're organized to put in the new transfer.

Installing the New Switch

You'll find out while purchasing for the present day transfer that now not all switches are alike within the way the wires are connected to it. Depending at the logo, type, and fashion of the switches, there are three techniques that the wires are related. Some switches may additionally have "pigtails" or wires already linked to them. Some should have the screws to connect the wires. Some can also need to have the holes inside the once more that the wires are inserted into, and some others can have every the screws and the holes to attach the wires to them. Any of those switches will art work to replace your antique transfer. The most effective difference is within the manner the wires connect to them.

Any of those switches will paintings to update your vintage transfer. The fine distinction is inside the way the wires connect with them. Which of these different types you purchase is based upon only on your personal preference.

If the type of transfer you acquire has the "pigtails", then, you could want wire nuts to attach them to the wires the vintage transfer modified into associated with. To join the "pigtails" to the wires, it's far now not vital to twist them collectively. All you need to do is positioned the stripped end of one of the wires in the mounting field collectively with the stripped prevent of the extraordinary "pigtail" twine and screw a cord nut onto them every. Then do the same with the alternative wires.

If the present day-day transfer has the screws, then bend the ends of the wires inside the mounting subject proper proper right into a hook-like shape if they may be now not already bent on this way. Then join the ideal wires to the right screws and tighten the screws to firmly preserve the wires in region.

If the today's switch has the holes in the again to connect the wires to, then ensure the wires in the mounting container have the stripped give up immediately. Then insert the nice wire into the proper hole to connect the wires to the switch.

If the switch has every the screws, and the holes, then you could connect the wires to the switch every way that you choose. Whichever way the wires are related to the modern-day day transfer, make sure that the switch is proper thing up earlier than you attach the wires.

As fast as you're finished attaching the wires to the trendy transfer, gently push the transfer and the wires decrease lower back into the mounting container. Then, insert the 2 mounting screws thru the switch's mounting bracket and into the holes within the mounting box and tighten them down snugly.

Make positive the transfer is centered in function so the quilt plate will in shape over it nicely. Then replace the cover plate and tighten the mounting screw snugly to maintain it in area. Never tighten the screws on the cover plate too tightly or it will crack the duvet plate. Once all this is finished, you may flip the circuit returned on and test the transfer. If the switch does no longer paintings, turn the circuit off once more and test to make certain the wires did now not come unfastened from the transfer or get damaged even as you have got been installing the transfer. If the transfer works, then your technique is completed.

Replacing a Switch with a Dimmer

To update a desired transfer with a dimmer transfer is completed in exactly the identical manner as while you're converting a general kind switch with every special. The fine difference is in the manner the dimmer transfer skills in contrast to the equal vintage kind switch. Since most dimmer switches come with the "pigtail" wires, you will need to put in it in the way previously described for putting in the ones type switches.

Chapter 9: How to Paint Your Interior

I: Tools and materials you'll need

II: Before You Begin

Before you begin the challenge of portray your private home or condo, you could need to perform a little things to put together your house for painting. First, you will need to get together all the gadget and substances that you may need for the interest. Refer to the gadget and materials list inside the starting of this section for the devices you may need for your pastime. Next, you can want to dispose of the fixtures from the rooms to be painted. If eliminating the fixtures from the rooms is inconvenient or not possible so that you can do, you may drift all of the furniture in every room into the center of the room and cover it with a drop material. Then you'll need to remove any images or different decorations from the walls. Remove any nails, screws, photo hangers or every other fasteners that can be on the walls. You'll additionally need to put off the curtains, curtain rods, blinds, or solar sun shades from the home windows as properly.

III: Preparing Your Walls

Before you may paint your partitions, you may need to scrub any dust and grease off them with an amazing purifier/stripper or the paint may not stick very well to the wall. If you have any stains that won't wash off the walls, you could want to use a stain killer/primer to the spots or they may bleed via the paint. You'll additionally want to patch any holes that can be in the walls from nails, screws, or different fasteners used to keep snap shots or different decorations. The next 3 sections of this section cowl a way to patch the numerous length holes you could have in your walls. They'll be blanketed one by one because every shape of hole, gouge, or dent requires a barely distinct approach to patching them.

Patching nail holes

Patching nail holes and considered one of a kind small punctures are the very high-quality wall damage to repair. For those styles of holes you will need a putty knife or small trowel, some spackling paste and a rag.

The first thing you'll want to do is to scrape any sticking out materials (paint, drywall, and so forth.) from around the edges of the holes. When you scrape those holes, keep the putty knife or trowel in order that the blade is at approximately a 30-degree perspective to the wall and pull it back towards the direction of the cope with. Never push it forward or you may turn out to be with a gouge in the wall. Once the sticking out material all through the holes have been scraped off, take a small amount of spackling paste out of its vicinity with a corner of the putty knife or trowel. While shielding the putty knife or trowel as flat in opposition to the wall as viable, push the spackling paste into the hollow with a scraping movement throughout the hole. Scrape any extra spackling paste off the wall and wipe away the rest of the more with the rag. Repeat this approach with all the nail holes and tremendous small punctures in all the partitions to be painted.

Patching holes up to a few" diameter

Patching holes big than nail holes up to a few" in diameter is a hint greater complicated than patching nail holes, however it is now not too tough to do. They do but; require a barely extremely good approach to patching them. For these holes you may need some patching plaster, a small trowel, a mixing container and combining spoon or stick, a sharp knife or razor blade, a newspaper, a drop cloth, and a rag.

First, spread the drop cloth out on the floor under the hollow to be patched. Then, use some protective tape to tape the drop fabric to the baseboard to preserve it from moving some distance from the wall. This is to prevent any plaster from getting on the ground. This is in particular critical if the ground is carpeted due to the reality plaster may be very difficult to get out of carpeting. Next, trim the difficult edges of the hollow to put off any loose plaster, paint, and drywall paper that might save you an extraordinary bond with the patch.

Use the sharp knife or razor blade to trim this cloth away. Brush any loose plaster quantities and plaster dirt away additionally. It's not important for the rims of the hollow to be perfectly clean. It's best crucial to eliminate any protruding or unfastened cloth.

If the hollow is anywhere from 1" to three" in diameter, it may be crucial to offer the hole with a backing to keep the plaster patch from falling into or out of the hollow in the route of the patching system. To do that, roll up a piece of newspaper to the approximate length of the hollow. Then twist it slightly to make it specially "spring like". Then insert it into the hollow until it reaches the opportunity aspect of the wall. Continue pushing it into the hole until it's far all the way in. Make fine that now not one of the newspaper is sticking out of the hole.

While doing this, make sure the newspaper presses firmly enough toward the other element of the wall and the once more edges of the hollow simply so it would not fall down internal of the wall. Now, mixture enough plaster to fill the hollow in keeping with the combination commands at the plaster package deal deal deal. Let it set until it reaches a thick pasty consistency. Now, even as the plaster is thickening, take a spray bottle full of cool, smooth water and spray around the edges of the hole, thoroughly wetting the plaster edges. This will help the plaster patch to bond with the wall and save you the plaster in the wall from drawing an excessive amount of moisture out of the patching plaster too speedy. As speedy because the plaster reaches the proper consistency, trowel it into the hole being careful no longer to push the newspaper withdrawing of its function behind the hole.

Now, easy the plaster patch out by way of protecting the trowel nearly flat towards the wall.

With the top edge of the trowel barely tilted out from the wall, use an upward motion across the patch. If the plaster sags after doing this, keep smoothing it out in the equal manner until it is organisation enough now not to sag. If on the equal time as you are smoothing it out it starts offevolved offevolved to crack or split, spray a few extra water on it and clean it out yet again.

Sometimes in huge holes like the ones made thru doorknobs, the plaster also can cut lower back a touch because it hardens leaving the patch with an indentation in it. If this takes vicinity you may want to use a 2d coat of plaster to it. Be effective to spray it with water earlier than making use of the second coat or it may now not adhere well to the primary coat. Because of a chemical reaction, the plaster will feel heat as it hardens. When it has completely hardened and now feels cool to touch, sand away any greater plaster with medium grit sandpaper.

Make wonderful you do not sand too much or you can need to workout greater plaster to the patch. Then smooth and mix the edges of the patch with best grit sandpaper. When this is completed and the patch is smooth and the edges are blended with the wall, it is ready to be painted. Gouges and dents may be filled in a comparable way except that they do not want the newspaper backing.

Patching large holes

Large holes require a totally unique technique to patching than the smaller ones do. If the hole is greater than three" or four" in diameter, it could now not be feasible to patch it using a newspaper backing and filling it with plaster as with the smaller ones. This is due to the fact in these big holes it will be almost no longer possible to get the newspaper backing to stay in area without falling down in the wall. This can sometimes be tough even in the smaller holes.

What you may need to do in the case of large holes, is to patch the hole the usage of a scrap piece of drywall that is the same thickness due to the fact the drywall in your partitions. To do this, you'll need to degree the thickness of your drywall. Before you may correctly diploma the drywall, you could need to make a clean component to diploma. Using a pointy software knife or first rate teeth determined blade, reduce away the ragged location at the bottom of the hole. Then, using a ruler or tape diploma, diploma the thickness of the drywall at the difficulty you narrow away. Be exceptional to install writing this measurement on a chunk of paper. If you don't have any suitable scraps of drywall lying around your private home or storage, as maximum humans do not, you can purchase a piece of drywall at your nearby home improvement hold.

Before you buy your drywall, you could need to apprehend the dimensions of the piece you could need. To find out the width and duration of the piece of drywall you can need, you can should prepare the hole for patching first. The following paragraphs provide an motive of the strategies for making geared up the hollow and using the patch.

Preparing the hollow

To put together the hole, you can should reduce it out big in a square shape. First, you may need to find out the studs on each facet of the hollow. This can be finished in numerous strategies. The simplest manner to do this is to apply an digital stud finder. These digital stud finders paintings with the beneficial aid of detecting the steel nails or screws used to lock the drywall to the studs. If you don't have a stud finder, you can use a sturdy magnet to locate the nails or screws inside the wall.

Another way, if you have a top notch ear, is to gently tap at the wall with a hammer over and over as you flow into throughout the wall. The sound it makes will exchange in pitch barely. For instance, inside the bays many of the studs, the sound can be a lower pitched hole sound. On the studs, the sound can be a better pitched extra robust sound. Another way is that if there may be an outlet or transfer masses much less than 16 inches from the hollow, there is probably a stud on one aspect of it or the opposite. This is due to the truth the mounting bins that the switches and stores are mounted in are set up to the studs.

One more way to discover the studs is, if the hole is large enough, you may reap in with a ruler or measuring tape and enlarge it to as a minimum one element until you hit the stud and study the dimension. Then repeat this for the alternative thing, moving the measurements to the outside of the wall with marks at the stud places. If you operate this approach, be very careful no longer to drop the ruler or measuring tape or you could lose it in the wall.

Once you have positioned and marked the stud locations, degree from the floor to the nice aspect of the hollow. Add 1" to this measurement and make a mark at the stud places on each element of the hollow. Using a right now aspect, draw a line between the ones marks with a pencil. Next, measure from the line you really drew to the lowest thing of the hole. Add 1" to this size and make a mark at both stud locations. Draw a line some of the ones marks. This will form the pinnacle and bottom borders of the patch hollow.

Connect those two strains collectively forming a rectangle as established beneath.

Make excellent that the lines are immediately and the corners are square (at 90-degree angles). This will help to insure that the patch will healthy in the hollow well. Now lessen the drywall out along the strains cautiously with a pointy software knife or observed, and put off the drywall from the hole. Now trim up and easy the top and bottom edges of the hole.

The aspect edges of the hollow are in fact flush with the studs and need to be cut decrease back ¾" to 1" greater to show sufficient of the studs to nail the patch to. Draw vertical traces parallel to the facet edges of the hollow ¾" to as a minimum one" from the edges. Carefully cut on the lines with a software program application knife and do away with the strips of drywall to reveal the studs. If there are any nails or screws exposed thru this technique, do away with them. Now trim up and clean the issue edges of the hole ensuring they will be right now and the corners are but rectangular. Now you can degree the period and width of the hollow for the patch.

Preparing the patch

Now which you have the measurements to your patch, you are organized to buy the piece of drywall you can need. Make satisfactory you get a piece of drywall massive than the patch so you'll have room for trimming and shaping the patch. It's fantastic to get a bit big sufficient to get or more patches out of it in case of mistakes in cutting out the patch. If your hollow isn't too large, you will be able to find out a scrap piece of drywall at the store. Some shops will deliver away these scraps freed from price.

Cut the piece of drywall to the measurements you took from the hollow. Make certain you chop it to in shape tightly in the hole. This will make filling the seams much much less hard. Once you've got were given the patch reduce out, region it in the hole to test for in shape. Trim and shape it to in shape if essential until it suits nicely in the hollow.

Applying the patch

Now that you have the patch lessen to healthy the hollow properly replace it inside the hollow and nail it in area with drywall nails. Put one nail in each nook and one every 3" aside on each components. When you nail it in region, angle the nails barely in the route of the studs so they'll hold better.

Be cautious while nailing or you could have every specific hole to patch. When the nail heads are flush with the floor, tap them in simplest a bit extra to form a moderate dimple inside the drywall. This is known as dimpling. This is finished to fill the dimple with plaster to cover the nail heads.

After this is completed, blend the patching plaster to fill the seams and dimples. Mix a small amount of plaster constant with the instructions on the plaster package deal deal. Mix the plaster till it has a thick soupy consistency. Spray a few cool, water over the vicinity with a twig bottle. Then trowel the plaster into the seams and dimples till they will be stuffed to a moderate mound. Let the plaster dry very well. Then using medium grit sandpaper, sand the seams flush with the wall and patch. Then, sand the seams and dimples clean with the notable grit sandpaper. Be cautious now not to sand an excessive amount of or you may sand the plaster out of the dimples. If you discover any gaps or air bubbles inside the seams or dimples, they may be full of spackling paste. After that is accomplished, you are prepared to start overlaying.

IV: Masking

The next step is to masks the entirety adjoining to the areas to be painted that you do now not need paint to get on. These matters may want to consist of any finished wooden surfaces along side: cupboards and cabinets, wood trim and moldings, wooden paneling, and so on. You'll additionally need to mask doorknobs, deadbolt locks, unpainted window trim, any non-detachable wall installation furniture, or wallpaper adjacent to a painted wall. Remove the duvet plates from the switches and stores and mask the switches and shops to hold paint from stepping into them. If you have got in no way had any revel in with overlaying, the subsequent paragraphs will deliver an reason for a way to try this with the severa surfaces and devices you can need to mask.

Cupboards and cabinets

Masking flat surfaces which encompass shelves and shelves is simple and clean to do. You'll want a deliver of three" masking tape and newspapers.

First, cautiously tear or reduce the pages of the newspaper apart on the creases. Now, lay an internet web page on a flat, smooth, and dry ground including a desk or counter and fold it in half the prolonged way. Next, tear or reduce off a chunk of covering tape about 2 inches longer than the length of the folded newspaper web web page. Position the tape on the point of the newspaper so the fold runs down the middle of the tape with approximately 1" of tape extending beyond the paper at both give up. Make high-quality there aren't any wrinkles within the paper or the tape and the tape is pressed down firmly at the paper. This is critical due to the fact wrinkles will permit paint to seep below the tape. Now the primary mask is ready and organized to be completed in your cabinet or cupboard.

Apply the masks to the cupboard or cupboard with the brink of the tape on the brink of the cabinet or cabinet. Make sure it's miles up to, but no longer on, the adjacent floor to be painted. Make positive the tape is without delay along the brink and covers the threshold truely. Also, make sure there aren't any wrinkles within the tape while utilizing it and it's far pressed down firmly so paint may not seep beneath it. Then tear off or three quick quantities of masking tape and tape the possibility facet of the newspaper masks to the cabinet or cabinet to keep it in area.

Now, put together the subsequent masks as described in advance and use it on the cupboard or cupboard in order that it overlaps the primary mask through manner of at the least 1". Then tape the overlapped edges of the two mask together leaving no areas wherein paint need to seep below.

Tape the opportunity thing of the mask to the cupboard or cupboard as you did with the primary mask. Repeat this manner until all edges of the cupboard or cabinet which may be adjoining to partitions to be painted are masked. Wood trim and moldings may be masked with the masking tape handiest except they're greater than 6" large.

Wood paneling

If you've got any walls which can be paneled, they will want to be masked on the aspect wherein the paneling meets the painted walls. If your paneled partitions are full-duration walls, (ground to ceiling) the threshold of the paneling that meets the painted wall will ought to be masked. This may be done in a comparable way as with the cabinets and cabinets. If you should paint the ceilings further to the walls, the paneled partitions will need to be in reality included to keep paint from dripping or splattering on them.

For this, it's far suggested that you use plastic drop cloths in desire to newspaper. To do that, spread out the drop cloth on the floor next to the paneled wall. Then pick out up the corner of the drop material, and with a small piece of shielding tape, tape it to the pinnacle edge of the paneling at one give up of the wall. Then go with the flow 2' or three' down the wall and area each extraordinary small piece of tape, keeping the plastic tight.

Continue in this way until you obtain the opportunity stop of the wall. Then even as the plastic drop fabric is in region, cross again and tape the pinnacle edge of the drop fabric all of the way at some point of leaving no gaps inside the tape. Tape the rims of the drop material to the edge of the paneled wall wherein it meets the painted wall. The paneled wall (or partitions) ought to be absolutely sealed off from any regions to be painted.

If your paneled walls are the kind that only goes element manner up the wall, there'll be a molding walking alongside the pinnacle edge of the paneling. You'll need to tape a drop fabric to the molding alongside the pinnacle side on the corner wherein the molding meets the wall. Be positive that the tape is pressed down firmly at the edge so if paint runs down and accumulates at this thing it may not seep beneath the tape.

Masking curved surfaces

In order to mask curved surfaces collectively with doorknobs, deadbolt locks, or slight furnishings, it will possibly be essential to apply a "wrap spherical" approach. For doorknobs, prepare a mask by manner of using folding a web net page of newspaper the long way. Then fold it all yet again the other way.

Now, workout a piece of tape to the lengthy aspect with the fold as you probable did with the mask for cabinets and shelves. Now fold the tape over to tape the 2 elements collectively. This will keep them together while you wrap it at some stage in the doorknob. Now exercise a 2d piece of tape to the equal element, but do now not fold this one over. Now, carefully observe the masks by way of using wrapping the taped aspect round the threshold of the spherical escutcheon plate. This plate suits up in the direction of the door. It's moreover once in a while referred to as a rose plate or flange plate. As you wrap the tape round this plate, be careful to hold the tape up against the painted surface of the door, but now not on the painted surface. After you have finished wrapping the masks across the doorknob, press the tape down firmly all of the way across the plate with a finger nail or tip of a flat blade screwdriver.

Now you've got commonplace a tubular mask throughout the doorknob. All it really is left to do is to twist the quit of the tube closed. If you choice, you can fold the twisted give up over and tape it, but it's not essential.

Deadbolt locks and rectangular escutcheon plates may be executed in a similar manner except the newspaper isn't wished. The tape can be wrapped round the brink of the plate forming a tube after which folded in to cowl the rest of the lock. Then a small piece of tape is delivered to the center to cowl any gaps in the tape.

Wall installation or ceiling hooked up mild furnishings additionally can be masked with this technique. All it honestly is essential is to do away with the globe or shade and wrap the three" overlaying tape across the out of doors of the fixture in a similar way as with the alternative round objects just cited.

V: Painting Your Walls

At this detail, all of the arrangements need to be entire. All the nail holes and every different holes ought to be patched and all of the covering need to be completed.

Now you need to spread drop cloths on the ground. It's not crucial to cowl all the flooring clearly on the identical time. This could possibly require the use of too many drop cloths and lift the price of your paint way. Instead, you can lay them out in a single room at a time, and then drift them from room to room as you go. If you have to paint quality the walls, you can lay out the drop cloth so it covers an area 3 to four ft from the partitions. If you'll paint the ceilings as properly, then you may want to cover the whole floor. When you lay out the drop cloths, tape them in place so that they won't bypass. If the ground is carpeted, tape the threshold of the drop fabric to the lowest of the baseboard.

If the floor is timber, tile, or linoleum, you may tape the drop material to the floor. If your baseboards are finished in area of painted, tape the drop material to the pinnacle edge of the baseboard to mask the baseboard further to cover the ground.

Now you are prepared to start portray. First, make certain your paint is mixed properly. Then pour simply sufficient paint into your curler tray to fill the reservoir cease of the tray. Now dip your corner curler into the paint and pull a small amount of paint up onto the angled "washboard" like region of the tray. Then roll the roller back and forth to get the paint lightly unfold throughout the roller and to dispose of the extra paint from it.

Then, begin with the useful resource of painting all of the corners among partitions, and some of the walls and ceilings. Next, paint the corners the diverse partitions and the woodwork (window trim, doorframes, and so on.). After this is completed, use the 3" trim curler or brush if critical to color the rest of the woodwork. Now, with the three" trim curler; paint a "problem" spherical every switch and outlet to help you avoid getting too close to them with the massive curler.

After all the corner and trim art work is finished, appearance it over cautiously to make sure you haven't disregarded any spots. When you're happy with the trim work you've got executed, you're organized to start portray the primary part of the walls. Dip your nine" curler into the paint on your tray and pull a small quantity of paint up onto the "washboard vicinity" as you in all likelihood did with the trim rollers. Roll it backward and forward to spread the paint across the roller frivolously.

For this method, you will want to add an extension address for your curler. Begin at one surrender of the wall. Use a sluggish upward stroke from the top of the baseboard as heaps due to the fact the ceiling. Then roll downward at a moderate mindset with the second stroke overlapping the primary stroke all the manner backpedal to the baseboard.

Rolling slowly on the number one 2 or three strokes after choosing up paint from the tray on every occasion will help save you the roller from splattering the paint. If you are not making plans to color the ceiling, be cautious no longer to touch it with the roller. Making full-duration strokes and overlapping them allows to prevent any left out spots between strokes. Every 3 or four strokes, or each time the roller begins offevolved offevolved to run dry, select up a few more paint from the tray as you probable did earlier than. As you paint your way at a few degree inside the wall, prevent every 3 or four ft and go decrease back over what you just painted all once more to smooth out any roller strains left within the returned of. Continue in this manner all of the manner throughout the wall.

After you have finished painting the partitions, in case your drop cloths are taped to the baseboards, you will need to take away the tape from them to colour the baseboards. If it is feasible, tuck the threshold of the drop cloth underneath the baseboards, then paint the baseboards with the three" trim roller or a brush. If it's far no longer feasible to tuck the drop cloth underneath the baseboards, then use a stiff piece of cardboard held at an attitude up in competition to the lowest of the baseboard to shield the ground. Then, the usage of a brush, cautiously paint the baseboard shifting the piece of cardboard along the baseboard as you flow.

If you recommend to shade the ceilings, then this ought to be finished first in advance than painting the partitions. Do this in a similar way as described formerly for the walls, with complete-period strokes in the course of the shortest duration of the ceiling. Don't save you until the entire ceiling of the room is painted. If you do, it will depart strains in the paint in which you stopped.

After you are completed with the painting, each at the give up of the day or at the give up of the hobby, make certain to easy your rollers and brushes right away. If you do not the paint will dry on them and they will be ruined. Be first rate to take away the curler covers from the rollers earlier than cleaning them or the paint gets indoors and dry, making it no longer feasible to get rid of the covers. Then wash them out very well. If you used a latex paint, you will simplest need water to clean them. If you used an oil-based totally paint, wash them out in the suitable thinner or solvent as encouraged at the paint area.

As quickly because the process is completed, remove all of the masking tape and newspaper from the masked surfaces carefully in an angular route a long way from the paint.

Chapter 10: How to Paint Your Exterior

I: Tools and Materials You'll Need

II: Before You Begin

Before you start portray the outdoor of your house, you may need to get collectively some or all the gadgets inside the phase "Tools and substances you may want" in the the the front of this phase. Which of the matters you'll want depends on the dimensions of your home and the man or woman of the device you need to do. For this reason, this a part of the phase will speak the precise types of paint jobs and the gadget and substances vital to do those jobs.

If you have got a unmarried story domestic, you can not want some of the items inside the listing. You might not need any tall extension ladders or scaffolds, so this form of project can be much much less tough and less difficult to do. The most effective ladders you'll need might be tall stepladders. Two 6' to 7' stepladders will normally be tall enough to assist you to acquire the eves of a unmarried tale domestic. Even if you're doing this hobby on my own, it is constantly an incredible concept to have tall stepladders. This way, if you should want a brief makeshift scaffold, you can placed or three planks among them on any step to form your scaffold. However, it is not encouraged putting the planks on the pinnacle two steps. When using ladders in this way, or some different manner, usually make sure the ladders have a robust footing and do not wobble.

It goes with out pronouncing you can need rollers and brushes, until you're making plans to spray paint. Spray painting can be protected in brief later in this phase. Brush and roller painting will in particular be included inside the ones sections as well.

Refer to the ones sections for delivered system and materials that you could want, in case you're planning to spray paint. You'll want roller trays and extension handles for the rollers. You'll moreover want drop cloths to cover any grass or flowers subsequent to the partitions of your own home. A paint scraper can also be had to scrape off any free, cracked, or peeling paint for your partitions. Wire brushes also can be wished for this reason. The relaxation of the devices on the listing also can be wanted for a unmarried tale home.

If your home is or extra memories tall, you will want tall extension ladders or scaffolds to will will let you advantage the second or 1/3 floor of your property. If you have no extension ladders or scaffolds, they'll be bought at a hardware hold or home development center. Some paint stores moreover deliver them. However, it is able to be more low-cost to rent the extra pricey gadget that you will be trying from an tool condo outlet. If you are making plans to spray paint your property, you could rent the spraying system moreover.

When buying the curler covers, make certain that they're the proper ones for the shape of siding you've got were given on your house. If your siding is a smoother sort of siding which embody clapboard, aluminum, or vinyl, a shorter nap curler cover with a ¼" to ½" nap will work well.

If your siding has a medium textured floor on the facet of stucco, or concrete, a thicker nap collectively with ¾" to at least one" will art work better. For carefully textured surfaces which include brick, it's miles best to use a deep-nap curler cover of 1" to 1½" deep pile.

For siding with overlapping edges, you can additionally need to apply a brush or trim roller to coloration the overlapped edges.

If your siding has a medium textured floor at the side of stucco, or concrete, a thicker nap which incorporates ¾" to as a minimum one" will paintings better. For cautiously textured surfaces which includes brick, it's miles notable to use a deep-nap curler cowl of one" to 1½" deep pile.

For siding with overlapping edges, you may additionally need to use a broom or trim curler to paint the overlapped edges.

Latex paints might also even permit moisture to pass thru them permitting condensation inside the wooden to get away with out harming the paint assignment. However, if the vintage paint is an oil-based paint, any condensation in the timber might not be capable of escape thru it or the cutting-edge layer of paint. Whichever type of paint you purchase ensure to take a look at the label to make certain it's miles the proper type for the ground it's far to be implemented to.

Masking tape will exceptional be important for covering exterior doorknobs, locks, and so forth. Unless you suggest to spray paint. In this situation, you could need to mask windowpanes and trim in addition to doorknobs and locks, and so on.

III: Preparations to Make

The arrangements are the most crucial steps in any paint technique. If the preparations aren't performed, or no longer finished very well sufficient, the paint hobby might not flip out properly, or won't ultimate prolonged.

The first detail you have to do to put together for the paint machine is, thoroughly have a study the entire outdoor of your own home for damage to the siding or trim that may prevent an awesome paint activity from lasting. Check for cracks inside the siding or damaged sections of siding. Check for cracked, peeled, or blistered paint as nicely. These paint conditions can advise a trouble with the siding underneath the paint that reasons these situations.

If the troubles within the siding that motive the ones paint conditions aren't repaired but absolutely repainted, those conditions will recur in the new paint interest. For instance, if the paint is peeling, how it's far peeling can imply the person of the trouble. If simplest the pinnacle layer is peeling, it is able to suggest that the surface of the vintage paint modified into not smooth. This trouble can be cured thru sanding and washing the vicinity in advance than making use of the modern-day paint. However, if the paint is peeling all of the way right down to the bare siding, this can suggest a terrible mission of priming all through the primary paint hobby. It may also advocate dust, grease, or a few one-of-a-kind distant places material have become on the siding earlier than the number one layer of paint changed into completed. This is why thorough preparations are most critical every time your house is painted.

If the paint is blistered, this can suggest moisture inside the siding beneath the paint. As the moisture vapors leave the siding, they pressure the paint to blister away from the siding. In any case, in case you find caution signs and symptoms of moisture in the siding below the paint, make certain to check for the cause of the moisture. There can be a leak in a water pipe inside the wall or a niche inside the siding that isn't sealed and moisture from rain, or dew, or a sprinkler machine has gotten into the siding. If that is the case, and your siding is a timber siding, then it could be critical to remove and replace this phase of siding.

If you do want to replace a section of siding, ensure to seal it with caulking to insure that this hassle does not stand up all over again in the new paint. In any case, all cracked, blistered, or peeling paint will have to be removed in advance than repainting your own home. This may be finished by means of sanding, or scraping, or scrubbing with a wire brush. If you have got have been given antique paint that has emerge as powdery, this may need to be removed as well or it's going to reason the ultra-modern paint to peel.

The next issue you can need to do is to ensure any loose dust, grease, dirt, or distinct foreign materials are thoroughly washed off with a solution of detergent and water. It's now not critical even though, to wash the complete house. Just the regions that is particularly dirty which includes regions close to the floor in which dirt and dust can splash up on the paint. Wash also out-of-the-manner regions together with beneath the eves or on windowsills and different such locations in which dust or grease will be predisposed to build up. The relaxation of the house may also actually be rinsed of with a garden hose.

While you are cleansing the ones grimy regions, test for mold stains as properly, but try not to confuse mildew with dirt. In a few cases, mold can appearance just like each unique spot of dirt. If you are now not positive whether or not or no longer or not an opening is dirt or mildew, you can check it via protecting a rag soaked with laundry bleach on it for a few minutes. If it's far mould, the spot gets lighter or nearly disappear. If it is dust, but, the spot will now not frequently alternate the least bit. Mildew is because of a fungus and can't be washed off as results as dirt. If you wash it off the equal manner as you're washing off dust, it can appear to clean off, however it'll come another time later after you have got were given finished repainting. To maintain it from coming lower back, you want to kill the fungus that reasons the mould. The exceptional way to do that is to scrub the region thoroughly with a mixture of bleach and TSP in water. Then permit the place dry completely.

Next, rinse the location with loads of clean water and allow it dry thoroughly. After the area is truly dry, test a stain blocker/primer to the area to prevent any mildew that stays from coming thru the modern day paint.

Another way to remove mildew is to sand it away with a disc sander attachment on an electric powered powered drill. However, this could high-quality paintings if the mold is on the ground of the paint. If the mold is in the wooden beneath the paint and is coming thru the paint, sanding it off may not get all of it. From the ground, it is actually not possible to tell if the mould is on the surface or within the timber under the paint. Therefore, if you plan to sand it off, you must make certain to use a stain blocker/primer to the region after sanding to make sure the mold might not come through the cutting-edge day paint.

The subsequent step is to check all caulked and puttied joints for cracked, broken or lacking caulk and putty. This might be one of the most crucial steps in making equipped your exterior for portray. If this step isn't taken, moisture may be able to get in in the back of the paint and purpose the paint to peel. It also can cause rotting inside the timber, in addition to cracking or warping and create masses greater paintings as a manner to repair within the close to destiny. Check to make sure that the joints around the window frames and doorframes in which they meet the siding are sealed with caulking and update any caulking this is chipped, broken, cracked, or lacking. Replace any window glazing that is faulty with new window glazing as properly.

If you have got have been given any damaged or cracked windowpanes, they need to get replaced earlier than you could paint those window frames. To get rid of the portions of broken glass, you can have to drag them out the use of a rocking motion even as pulling. This might be most regular in case you put on thick paintings gloves at the equal time as casting off the damaged glass.

Once all of the glass has been removed, you could need to remove the vintage window glazing with the resource of scraping and chipping with a putty knife or chisel. If the vintage putty is to tough to get rid of in this manner, strive applying a few heat to the putty with a propane torch or a blow dryer set on, warm. The blow dryer also can make the effort to soften the putty, but you'll be much less probable to burn the wood window frame or set your home on fireside. If you choose out to use the propane torch, make sure to have a hearth extinguisher or a bucket of water on hand without a doubt in case. However, the author strongly recommends using the more constant approach with the blow dryer. After the vintage putty has been eliminated, you could degree for the ultra-modern glass.

Before you positioned in the cutting-edge windowpane, make a check in shape to ensure the windowpane fits properly.

If the windowpane fits properly, eliminate it another time and put together to put in it within the frame. For a wood frame, coat any naked timber with an outside primer to seal the wooden. Next, roll out an extended bead of the window-glazing compound until it's about 1/8" in diameter. Then press it into the rabbet. The rabbet is the groove into which the glass fits. Now place the windowpane in function and press it toward the glazing compound tough sufficient to flatten the compound. Don't worry approximately the extra compound that squeezes out round the edges. This will assist in forming a seal.

Now you can want to install glazing elements. These are small triangular portions of steel that keep the glass in vicinity. This is performed via pushing them in with the brink of a putty knife. If the timber is certainly too hard to push them in, then you can cautiously tap at the putty knife with a hammer. You'll want to use or greater on each side.

Now to complete sealing the window, roll out a few other prolonged bead of the glazing compound until it's far 3/8" to 1/2" in diameter and press it into region spherical all 4 factors of the windowpane. Then scrape the excess off and form a bevel within the compound by means of way of way of dragging the putty knife throughout it at approximately a 45-degree mindset ensuring the putty tightly meets every the glass and body.

You need to furthermore take a look at for any uncovered rusty nail heads that could have labored their manner unfastened. If you find out any of those, you'll need to countersink them. That is, pound them lower returned in till the heads are surely underneath the ground of the timber with a hammer and a nail set. If the nails have huge heads that can not be countersunk, you'll want to both replace them with nails that can be countersunk consisting of finishing nails, or sand the rust off the heads and notice-excessive them. If you countersink the nails, fill inside the countersink with wooden putty and allow the putty to dry earlier than painting.

It's additionally an superb idea to check for every other issues that could purpose moisture to get within the returned of the paint and motive cracking or peeling of the fashionable paint, which incorporates leaking or clogged rain gutters and downspouts. As you test the ones, search for any streaks on the winning paint. This is an indication that they may be clogged or leaking. Make sure they're wiped smooth out and restore any leaks in them in advance than using the latest paint.

As a rule, it is fine to take down the rain gutters and downspouts earlier than you paint the trim to allow less difficult get admission to to the surfaces underneath them. While you've got got them down, you may test for any cracks, or holes, or leaking seams that can be gift and determine whether or now not to patch or replace them. If you are making plans to color them as nicely, having them down will make painting them lots less complex. You can lay them out the other way up on drop cloths and paint them. Make positive they are thoroughly wiped clean and free of any rust (if they may be steel) in advance than you paint them.

IV: Painting the Walls

After making all the arrangements, it is an superb concept to make a final inspection to make sure you haven't not noted something. A unmarried ignored unsealed joint within the siding can reason quite a few harm to the paint, timber, masonry, and drywall that you may must restore later. If moisture gets into this unsealed joint, it can reason the paint to blister and peel. Worse, it may purpose the wood to crack, swell and cut up, warp, or maybe rot out. It can purpose the drywall on the interior of the wall to swell, rot and collapse if the moisture gets at the back of the moisture barrier. It can also purpose deterioration and cracking of your masonry as nicely. All of a good way to require huge as well as high-priced restore art work. If you have got any unsealed joints most of the siding and a window body, moisture must get into the timber of the window body. This have to motive the wooden to swell or warp, that might purpose the windowpane to crack or damage. If this takes place, you could want to replace the window frame.

When you have got got finished making your inspection and you're satisfied that all crucial preservation and arrangements have been made, it is time to move straight away to the challenge of making use of the paint.

When buying your paint, it's miles wonderful to buy all the paint you'll want for the entire task at one time, ensuring that the batch numbers on all of the containers are the equal. Different batch numbers endorse barely one-of-a-type shades inside the color. So, buying it all at one time with the same batch numbers will help to insure that every one the containers of paint will in form with every one in every of a type. This is particularly real even as the use of a colour apart from white.

Painting the outdoors of your own home will take several gallons of paint. Of direction, the quantity of paint wanted will depend upon how big your own home is, and whether or not or now not or no longer or no longer you're painting the complete residence.

To discover about how an lousy lot paint you may need on your paint hobby, you can must determine out the rectangular photographs of the outside surfaces of your house to be painted. This would require measuring the height and period of each wall or floor to be painted. Then multiply the ones measurements to get the square snap shots of the ground. For example, a wall 8 toes excessive and 20 ft prolonged may be 160 square toes in place (8 x 20 = one hundred sixty).

To calculate the area of a tapered wall under a gabled roof, degree the width of the wall at the problem the taper starts offevolved. Then degree the height of the tapered area, from the middle of that line as masses as the peak. Multiply then divide with the aid of 2 (see example below).

If you're planning to coloration most or your complete houses outdoor you can want severa gallons of paint. Paint may be sold in severa sizes of bins, but for large jobs that require more than 3 or 4 gallons, it's miles exceptional to shop for it in five-gallon buckets. This way it's miles greater affordable and less hard to discover sufficient containers with matching batch numbers.

Before you begin to follow the paint, make certain to thoroughly mixture each container of paint as it's used. Because most of the pigment settles to the bottom of the field, it is going to be critical to pour some of the paint proper into a blending bucket. Then combination the last contents of the container till all of the pigment on the lowest may be very properly combined. Then pour the mixed paint into the aggregate bucket with the relaxation of the paint you poured off and blend once more. You can also moreover additionally then pour the combined paint lower lower lower back into the specific field or use it out of the combination bucket.

When making use of the paint, it is great to start at the pinnacle and paintings down. This way, you won't run the danger of messing up the moist paint as you will if you worked from bottom to top.

Paint the number one a part of the partitions first and shop the trim artwork for very last. The cause for that is that it's miles much less complex to manipulate the smaller trim rollers or brushes greater exactly than it's miles to govern the bigger rollers. For instance (in case you paint the trim first), even as you paint the number one part of the wall next to the trim it's going to possibly be nearly now not possible to keep away from getting paint at the freshly painted trim. If the trim is carried out very last, it will in all likelihood be lots much less complicated to keep away from getting the trim paint at the primary part of the wall using a broom.

If you're planning to spray paint, you could need to masks the trim, home home home windows, and doorways to prevent over spray from getting on them. You'll additionally want to thin the paint substantially in order for it that allows you to be sprayed. Refer to the thinning commands at the paint bins, for guidelines for spray painting.

If you're painting your home thru your self or with only one helper, the extraordinary concept may be to color one aspect of the residence at a time. Paint the precept a part of the wall beginning at the pinnacle and running down, then paint the trim, window frames, doorframes, and some exceptional trim your home may have. Then waft to the subsequent wall or side of the residence and paint it on this equal manner. This way you can maintain your self some time and artwork moving ladders and drop cloths and one-of-a-type gadget and factors to and fro. If you do a part of the challenge at one time and plan to do the relaxation later, this way as a minimum the walls you have got finished are whole.

V: Painting the Trim

The great device for painting the trim is a broom 2" to a few" large with an angled tip. Use the two" brush for slim areas and the three" brush for the wider regions of the trim and any painted doors. If you've got were given any trim along with the "grids" in some window frames, a 1" brush will work extraordinary. In a few domestic development shops and paint shops, paintbrush devices to be had that embody

1", 2", and three" brushes. Whether you purchase them one after the other or in a difficult and fast, make certain that they've the angled suggestions. The angled tip gives you higher manipulate of the brush and it's far a more bendy brush than the rectangular tipped brushes.

Trim rollers and corner rollers will paintings for some of the broader trim, but, brushes continuously paintings nice for the window trim paintings. When painting window frames, specially window frames with grids, it can not be finished with a roller. Begin at the top of the window frame and paint cautiously round the edges of the frame wherein they meet the wall. Be cautious not to have too much paint on the comb or it will drip at some stage in you and the wall.

Next, paint the inner frame regions next to the glass the use of a 1" brush. Be careful no longer to get too much paint at the glass. If you do, you'll should wait till it dries after which scrape it off with a window scraper or razor blade. Next, paint the rest of the window frames a number of the 2 regions you simply painted.

Painting doorframes is similar to painting window frames. Begin on the top and paint the edges of the doorframe in which it meets the wall. Then paint the internal edges after which the precept a part of the frames. If the doorways are to be painted as nicely, they'll be painted with a curler, inside the event that they have got a flat ground. If the door has a paneled format, then a broom may be had to paint any decorative or textured regions. If the door has simplest a minimum amount of texture, which includes with a simple paneled door, a deep-nap curler will do the manner. If you have louvered shutters, the best manner to shade them is to take them down and spray-paint them.

However, in case you're painting with the resource of hand, then a broom is the higher tool for the interest. They can also be painted in place at the same time as being painted by using manner of brush. Cornices and unique trim must be painted with a brush as well.

When portray cornices and specific trim with difficult to reap areas, it's far high-quality to shade inner the ones hard to advantage areas first. This is due to the truth at the equal time as you push the brush into those areas, it'll depart beads of paint at the out of doors edges of these regions.

Once you've got completed painting the inner hard to reap areas, you could paint the outer edges. Then paint the back and front edges, even as the paint beads round the rims are nevertheless moist. This will easy them out and save you them from walking.

NOTE: Any paint beads or runs that have been present inside the previous paint jobs should had been sanded off finally of the schooling segment of the venture. If they have been ignored in the route of the arrangements, this need to be performed in advance than you start painting this trim or they'll display through the ultra-modern paint interest.

Trellises should furthermore be painted using a 2" angled tip brush. However, when you have trellises that have vines developing on them, you can or might not need to colour them. If there are only a few vines then you'll be able to paint spherical them or circulate them over slightly as you paint.

If your trellises are full of vines, then you definately probably should now not repaint them the least bit unless you need to remove all the vines first. Be fine to do not forget in case you need to take away the vines, as it will take a long time for them to grow lower lower back.

If your trellises are damaged, rotting, or broken, you may need to replace them with new ones. In this example, you may most probable must reduce down the vines to take away the vintage trellises. In a few times, whilst the vines are not too thick or interwoven into the trellis, the vines can be eliminated without being lessen down. To do this, cautiously untangle the vines from the trellis one after the opportunity, beginning on the pinnacle and working all of the manner right right down to the ground. Lay each vine out on the floor being careful no longer to interrupt them. After all the vines have been eliminated, the antique trellis can now be replaced. Remove the screws or nails mounting the trellis in place, and then cast off the vintage trellis.

It's pleasant to paint the modern-day-day trellis earlier than mounting it in place.

The new trellises have to be spray painted, first, with an incredible primer/sealer, then with the end shade. This is to ensure that the first coat of paint the current trellises get maintain of will cover truly and seal the wooden to protect it from the climate and untimely rotting. If you can't spray paint the new trellises, then paint them with a 2" brush and ensure you cover the timber honestly with the primer/sealer coat after which the surrender coloration after it dries thoroughly. When they may be dry, you can mount them in region where the antique ones were.

Then, one by one update the vines on the trellises. You can do that in strategies. You can both cautiously re-tangle them on the trellises by way of way of weaving them onto it, or you may do no a good deal less than weaving the vines outside and inside of the trellises and tie the majority of the vines. The author recommends the later of the two because it'll do the least amount of damage to the vines. Later as the vines grow they will entangle themselves inside the trellises and then the strings can be removed.

Before painting the eves, make certain to dispose of the antique rain gutters and put together the surfaces for portray. Fill all the mounting holes with wood putty. Then thoroughly coat all surfaces of the eves with an incredible primer/sealer before the usage of the stop color. This is in particular essential if you have a hassle at the side of your gutters clogging or leaking. If the wooden could now not have an excellent seal, the eves have to usually tend to rot out in locations inflicting you to should update them in advance. When you replace the rain gutters, it is incredible to replace them with new ones, especially if the vintage ones leaked.

Once all the trim is completed, you are equipped to move at once to the following wall. At this factor you could both; easy up and save you the interest until you've got got time to shade the subsequent element of your private home, or circulate your tool round to the following issue of your own home and clean up for the day. It's typically notable to start a glowing wall on a easy day.

After all the partitions and trim are painted, you may start the very last easy up with the aid of way of using pouring any paint left over from the combination bucket or roller trays returned into the ideal containers and seal them up tight. Then very well smooth all of your rollers and brushes. Be advantageous to cast off the roller covers from the rollers earlier than cleaning or they'll come to be absolutely stuck on the rollers. If you used a latex paint, clean up may be an clean activity. All you could need is water with a small quantity of detergent added. If you used an oil-primarily based completely paint, ensure to smooth your rollers and brushes with the solvent or thinner endorsed by using the usage of manner of the paint manufacturer.

Next, remove any overlaying that could though be on your property, and fold up all of the drop cloths. If all the preparations have been finished successfully, you need to be able to experience your new paint system for numerous future years. However, in case you missed any leaks, or capability condensation issues, or vital safety in advance than you painted your house, you may must do that activity over again masses quicker. So, ensure you're most thorough on the identical time as you are doing the initial inspection and education degrees of this hobby.

Chapter 11: How to Fix or Replace a Leaky Faucet

I: Tools and Materials You'll Need

II: My Faucet is dripping

Drip...Drip...Drip..."Ugh...Yawn...What's that noise? Oh no! My faucet is dripping! I'll by no means get any sleep now!" Drip...Drip...Drip... "Oh what can I do?" Drip...Drip...Drip... "I comprehend! I'll located a rag inside the sink to lure the drops."

Drip...Drip...Drip...Splat...Splat...Splat...
"Oh no, that may not work!" Drips...Drip...Drip... "Yes, I'll stick the rag up the faucet to plug it up!" Drip...Drip... "Yes, it definitely is have been given it!"........................Drip...Drip...Drip... "Oh no, now not over again!" Drip...Drip...Drip... "What time is it? It's too past due to call a plumber. What am I going to do?"

Is this a familiar scenario? Most folks have skilled a few element like this at one time or some distinctive in our lives. Some human beings have professional it extra instances than we care to consider. Now, with the assist of this phase you will be prepared, and understand truly what to do the subsequent time you discover yourself on this situation.

The previous scenario, in most times, has a quick and easy short restore, to help you get decrease lower back to sleep. Under all sinks mounted on the wall, there are "deliver valves", one for decent, and one for cold water. Each may also have a small flexible tube coming out of the top and going as tons as the faucet. This flexible tube referred to as a "riser" can be crafted from metal or plastic. These "deliver valves" and "risers" are what deliver the faucet with water.

Feel the drops to peer whether or no longer they're heat or bloodless. Then, discover the deliver valve that materials whichever side is dripping. Then turn it off through twisting the manage in a clockwise course till the dripping stops. If you can not inform with the useful resource of the texture of the drops whether or not the new or cold is dripping, then turn one off and notice if the dripping stops. If the dripping keeps for greater than a minute or , then turn it lower lower again on and flip the opposite one off. If the dripping still keeps, then every the today's and cold taps can be leaking, or the supply valves may be leaking.

To check this, flip every deliver valves off. If the supply valves are not defective the dripping will stop. Now you will be capable of get a extremely good night time time's sleep. In the morning you could make the crucial maintenance to stop the dripping.

In most cases, you may want to change a washer. In a few instances but, the hassle may additionally furthermore lie with a defective valve or valve seat. In any case, all of these elements are with out problems available at your community hardware, plumbing deliver, or domestic improvement shops.

The rest of this section will cover the techniques for changing a bathing system inside the maximum common sorts of faucets.

The Two Handle Faucet

To exchange a washer, the number one issue you may need to do is make certain every deliver valves are have become really off. After turning them off, open each the latest and cold faucets one after the other. This accomplishes matters. (1) It relieves any water strain in the risers and taps so you can get rid of the valves without water squirting all over. (2) It enables to diagnose a defective deliver valve. For example, if after turning off each supply valves and turning at the latest water tap, the water continues running slightly for severa seconds then the current water deliver valve is faulty. If the water stops after some seconds, then the state-of-the-art water supply valve is strolling well. Then, activate the bloodless water tap. If the water maintains taking walks for some of seconds, then the bloodless water supply valve is defective. If the water stops, then the cold water supply valve is walking properly. If every of the supply valves is faulty, then the faulty valve will should be replaced. This can be blanketed in phase IV "What if the supply valves are frozen". Refer to this segment and accurate the deliver valve problems in advance than continuing directly to replace the washers.

The subsequent step in changing the washing machine is to eliminate the tap contend with from the valve that is leaking. In the maximum common kinds of faucets, a Phillips head screw on the pinnacle holds on the cope with. The screw is usually hidden below a ornamental cap with an "H" or a "C" on it. Pry off the cap with a flat blade screwdriver. Then remove the Phillips head screw. Now the address should without issues elevate off of the valve stem. If it's miles stuck because of corrosion, lightly pry it loose from below with the issue of the flat blade screwdriver with one hand whilst lifting it with the other hand as tested below.

In some unique forms of taps a setscrew on the factor, usually close to the bottom holds at the cope with. To cast off the ones ought to require both a small flat blade screwdriver or a small Allen wrench, relying on the shape of setscrew used. Loosen the setscrew, but do no longer eliminate it. Then boost the address off within the identical manner as with the preceding kind.

The next step is to put off the valve. For this you may need each a channel lock pliers or a crescent wrench. Under the manage you'll discover a hex nut across the valve stem. This hex nut is called a "packing nut". Some sorts of taps may have a locknut in vicinity of the packing nut. Unscrew the packing nut and slide it off of the valve stem.

If your tap has a locknut in preference to a packing nut, you can understand the difference at a look. The locknut may be rounded with flat sides for gripping with a wrench as confirmed below.

In some of the ones varieties of faucets the valve stem also can come out with the locknut. This will now not interfere with the changing of the bathing system. However, if your tap leaks from below the take care of at the same time as grew to emerge as on, the O-ring can also need to get replaced. In this situation, you can want to cast off the locknut from the valve stem to facilitate the removal and opportunity of the O-ring.

The washer is placed at the lowest end of the valve stem. Depending on the sort of tap you've got were given, it will probable be held in region every with the resource of a washing machine screw, a stem nut, or the forestall of the stem. In the number one two instances, the bathing tool is eliminated by unscrewing the bathing device screw or stem nut. Then the showering device may be eliminated from the sleeve into which it suits. If the bathing machine does now not come out of the sleeve with out hassle, then lightly pry it out thru setting the top of a screwdriver into the screw hollow in the center of the showering device. Be careful not to harm the sleeve whilst eliminating the washer or you may need to replace the valve stem as properly.

In the 1/3 case, in which the bathing machine is held in region by means of manner of the stop of the stem, the stem have to be removed from the valve body. To do this, preserve close to the square protrusion on the surrender of the stem with more than one pliers and unscrew the stem from the valve frame. Remove the washing machine and update it with a modern one of the equal length and form. Then screw the valve stem lower back into the valve body.

Now, earlier than screwing the valve yet again into the faucet, take a look at the valve seat for put on or damage. If the seat is worn or damaged, you will want to update it earlier than you reassemble the faucet. To do away with a valve seat, you'll want a valve seat wrench. This is an "L" fashioned steel rod with a couple of hex heads on every ends. Simply insert one give up or the opposite into the hole within the seat till you locate the size that suits. Then unscrew and take away the seat. Screw the modern-day seat in its location. Now you could reassemble the tap.

After you've got reassembled the tap, make sure each taps are grew to emerge as off absolutely. Then turn the deliver valves decrease lower returned on and look ahead to any leaking or dripping from the spout.

If there's any leaking from under both of the handles, you'll want to disassemble that tap and take a look at to make sure the packing or O-ring isn't broken or out of place. If there may be any dripping from the spout, you can need to test the washing device and valve seat all over again to ensure they'll be in outstanding condition and assembled efficiently. If after a few minutes you do no longer see any leaking or dripping, you then have correctly everyday your faucet.

Single Handle Lever Faucets

Most single deal with lever kind faucets will very last for severa years with out the need for servicing. When this sort of faucets starts offevolved offevolved leaking or dripping, in some instances, the entire faucet may additionally additionally additionally need to get replaced. This is because of the truth it is either an unserviceable layout, or alternative factors may be tough to attain. In some times you could ought to supply for the elements from the manufacturer, that may take numerous weeks. Other designs of those taps are serviceable and components are more easily obtained. Two of the more common kinds of those taps can be mentioned right proper here.

The Ball Valve Faucet

In this sort of faucet, a ball with 3 passages thru which the water flows whilst the faucet is grew to come to be on, acts as the valve. When the deal with is lifted up and targeted, the ball valve is located with all three passages lined up with the three ports within the valve frame. This permits each heat and cold water to waft and blend. The resulting warmth water then flows via the spout. When the manage is shifted to one aspect or the possibility, the go with the go along with the float costs of the brand new and bloodless water is modified to govern the temperature of the water. When the deal with is moved all the manner right down to the off characteristic, the passages within the ball valve are moved out of alignment with the ports inside the valve body, slicing off the go along with the go together with the float of the water.

Repairing this form of faucet is tremendously clean. First, as with each faucet repair jobs, make sure the supply valves are grew to come to be all of the way off. Then raise the manipulate to the complete "on" characteristic to launch the water stress. This may also placed the manage within the proper role to provide you higher get proper of entry to to the setscrew that holds on the control. This setscrew may also furthermore have every a slotted head or an Allen head (counting on the producer). So you may want either a small flat blade screwdriver or an Allen wrench to loosen it. Loosen the setscrew sufficient to launch the control, however do no longer remove the setscrew absolutely. It can be very small and may be misplaced easily. Now put off the cope with from the tap.

Beneath the contend with you may find out the valve cap. Unscrew the cap and put off it. Under the cap is a limiter cam, which limits the movement of the address. Pull out the stem of the ball. Along with the stem the limiter cam, rubber seal, and ball valve will pop out.

If the faucet turned into leaking from the lowest of the address, then the rubber seal will want to get replaced. If the faucet become dripping from the spout, then the two rubber valve seats and seat springs inside the valve body will want to get replaced. Remove the valve seats and comes carefully with a pair of needle nostril pliers. Both the rubber seats and seat springs have to get replaced. Because the fault can be each with worn or broken seats, or prone seat springs. Insert the new seats and springs with the aid of the use of manner of pressing them in in conjunction with your finger. This manner the pliers will no longer harm them.

Replace the ball valve in the valve body, making sure that the manual pin at the internal of the valve frame fits right into a slot inside the ball. Then replace the rubber seal (with a brand new one if critical) on top of the ball. Next, insert the limiter cam, ensuring that the tab on the factor suits into the slot on the valve body. Now, screw the cap lower once more at the valve frame. Turn the deliver valves back on and flow into the stem of the ball to the "on" characteristic. Check for any water leaking across the stem.

If there can be any leaking, you may want to tighten the adjusting ring at the cap with a screwdriver in a clockwise direction until the leaking stops. If the deal with moves with hassle after the leaking is stopped, the limiter cam and seal will each want to get replaced. If the cope with moves with out issue, then reattach the deal with making sure the setscrew is tightened firmly.

Disk Cartridge Faucet

This form of faucet is quite clean to repair. After turning off the supply valves, elevate the cope with up all of the manner to launch the water strain. Under the lever you may locate the setscrew. Loosen the setscrew however do no longer take away it. Then improve the deal with off of the faucet. If your tap has a drain plug address, you will need to disconnect the rod under the sink. First, mark the place of the thumbscrew with a marker or a bit of tape. Then disconnect the rod and pull it up out of the faucet. Next, unscrew the 2 Phillips screws on the lowest of the faucet that hold the tap cover in region, and then take away the duvet.

If your faucet does no longer have those two screws, then a retainer ring under the deal with will maximum likely keep on the cover. Unscrew this ring to remove the duvet. Once the quilt is remover, you will see the valve cartridge. This is commonly held in place with the useful resource of two screws. Remove those screws after which the cartridge. Replace the cartridge with a contemporary one, making sure it is positioned correctly.

Reattach the faucet cowl and cope with. Insert the drain plug manage and rod inside the top of the faucet and reconnect the rod and thumbscrew inside the feature marked with the aid of the marker or tape. After you've got were given reassembled the tap, flip the supply valves on all over again and test for any leaking or dripping. If there can be any leaking or dripping, you may need to disassemble the faucet once more and check the cartridge to ensure it is set up effectively. If it become installation efficaciously however despite the fact that leaks, then the ultra-modern cartridge may be defective and need to be decrease back to the shop and exchanged.

www.ingramcontent.com/pod-product-compliance
Lightning Source LLC
Chambersburg PA
CBHW071442080526
44587CB00014B/1956